Keep On The Sunny Side

REFLECTIONS ON LIFE'S JOURNEY

LILA JOSEPH

RIPE PUBLISHING

ALSO BY LILA JOSEPH

From the Prairie to the World

Published by Ripe Publishing, P.O. Box 1731, La Mirada, CA 90637.

Unless otherwise specified all Scripture verses are from the King James Version (public domain).

Editors: Mark Joseph, D.J. Nielsen
Cover Design: Linda Tazberikova
Interior Design: D.J. Nielsen, Toni Burge
Editorial assistance: Kathy Brubacher, Bobb Joseph, Bethany Thompson, Pam Watson

ISBN: 978-0-9827761-5-5

Printed in the United States of America

Keep On The Sunny Side

REFLECTIONS ON LIFE'S JOURNEY

CONTENTS

Contents

Contents

CHAPTER SEVENTEEN

Goodbyes 91

CHAPTER EIGHTEEN

Service With a Smile 96

CHAPTER NINETEEN

Free at Last 106

CHAPTER TWENTY

Back in Japan 111

CHAPTER TWENTY-ONE

The Last Time 114

APPENDIX

Selected Poems by Lila Joseph 123

There's a dark and a troubled side of life;
There's a bright and a sunny side, too;
Tho' we meet with the darkness and strife,
The sunny side we also may view.

Keep on the sunny side, always on the sunny side,
Keep on the sunny side of life;
It will help us every day, it will brighten all the way,
If we keep on the sunny side of life.

Tho' the storm in its fury break today,
Crushing hopes that we cherish so dear,
Storm and cloud will in time pass away,
The sun again will shine bright and clear.

Keep on the sunny side, always on the sunny side,
Keep on the sunny side of life;
It will help us every day, it will brighten all the way,
If we keep on the sunny side of life.

Let us greet with a song of hope each day,
Tho' the moments be cloudy or fair;
Let us trust in our Savior always,
Who keepeth everyone in His care.

–Ada Blenkhorn / Howard Entwisle

CHAPTER ONE

This World Is Not My Home

Life is full of choices, and each choice takes us on a different path. The path that led me to become a missionary and eventually took me to Japan started with my Grandparents' decision to come to America. As I look back on that and many other decisions, I can see God's hand of preparation for the unusual paths my family would take.

For the first seven years of my life I lived near a town called Schafer in North Dakota. My Dad homesteaded there, and in the earlier years it was a booming Midwest town. But then the railroad came through and bypassed Schafer, going to a town called Watford City. Schafer then became a ghost town, which is how I remember it.

Both sets of my grandparents left their native lands, cultures, languages, and relatives to travel to a distant country with a new culture, new language, and few, if any relatives. It must have been daunting to travel in those days, and then to settle in new areas and with so few conveniences that we think we can't live without today.

Dad's parents emigrated from Norway and settled in Iowa, where Grandpa became well-to-do working in the lumber business. My eldest brother, Clarence, remembers him coming home in his horse-drawn carriage wearing white gloves, as his hired helpers unhitched the horses and took them to their barns. He was also a lay preacher, and the story goes that once some men knelt in the road in front of his house in mockery of him. Not long afterward, one of them lost a child and he asked Grandpa to officiate at the funeral.

Dad left behind all of this in answer to the "Go west, young man!" phrase coined by the newspaper editor Horace Greely that was commonly heard at the time, encouraging America's Westward expansion. Dad arrived in Williston, North Dakota, and stood on the platform wondering if he should go farther west, where many settlers had gone, or go east to Schafer. He went east, and it was there where they had a revival which eventually touched our family and changed the outcome of our lives forever.

I never thought Dad felt sorry that he had left so much behind in Iowa. He loved the West all his life. He took off from his native Iowa as a young twenty-something man, leaving behind a prosperous family business to pioneer as a homesteader. After getting his land, he built a sod house which became his first home. He used to say that America knew North Dakota was a pain in the neck, but when oil wells began springing up all over the state, they knew it was growing pains.

Dad's jokes were usually on himself or his state, like the one about the lady who with her husband was visiting the area and swung her arm over the vast plains and said, "I'd have to love my husband an awful lot to live here!"

Another of his favorites was recounting the time some ranchers and farmers were lined up for something that required them to give their name. "Kringlaak, Severson, Finsaas…" and finally the man looked up and admonished, "Why don't you men get white men's names?"

Even as a child, I recognized that my Dad was a great storyteller and entertainer. During wheat threshing season, the farmers helped each other, so usually a crew of eight to ten would go from farm to farm helping each other out. The women made great feasts, so it was a fun time for everyone. I distinctly remember the men coming in and settling in for their hand-washing and eating, but when Dad came in, the place livened up. He was always full of stories and he never embellished them. I can't tell you how many times I heard the story of the murder of an entire family and the lynching that ensued!

Mother's family also emigrated from Norway, where she was born. She was eight years old when the Aarhus family left their homeland and came to America, landing in Nova Scotia, Canada, then traveling by train to Iowa, where they had relatives. In a short time, they also felt the pull to the West, and Grandpa Aarhus went on ahead to Schafer, where he homesteaded, and then Grandma and the rest of the family joined him. When Mother was about 17, she took a job at a hotel in Schafer. During this time she and Dad met and both were with other friends when Dad changed seats in the car so he could be near Mom. Eventually, they were married in a ceremony at her parents' place and began their life together in humble surroundings, becoming a vital part of the early settlers who blazed a pioneering trail.

Mother remembers Dad's Mother as a godly woman, judging from her letters to her son and family in the far West. Dad's father, was a carpenter from Norway, where some of his buildings still stand, so it wasn't long before he built a big house on their land.

CHAPTER TWO

After Seven Boys...

After seven boys, I was born. For my parents, I'm sure it was like a prize in the midst of the worst depression America has ever known, to finally have a daughter. Growing up I never felt strange that I didn't have sisters. Nor did I feel I was overly spoiled, though I do remember when I didn't get my way I'd head for a bed and cry, which would then cause Dad to come and get me. I also remember that at some point he stopped intervening, and I had to shape up by myself! I would go stand behind his rocking chair, though, when I got in trouble. That was a safe place and no one dared touch me. When I was four or five, Dad went to Iowa to his mother's funeral, and one night I cried because I missed him.

But my earliest memory was when I was two years old, and my brother Marvin lifted me up to see my little sister, Helen Arlene, who had died soon after birth, in her casket. I always wondered what it would have been like to have had a sister.

It was around this time that Mom became very sick—her sister Alma said they expected to hear of her death at any time—but then she had a life-changing encounter with the Lord that brought her back to health and changed her life forever. She made a bargain with God as she languished near death in the hospital, promising Him that if He would heal her, she would give her life to Him and serve Him, though she knew it would be hard because Dad was very anti-Christian. It seemed like he tried to leave spiritual things behind when he left his family in Iowa. Before long, Mom got well, went home, and from then on became a strong Christian, and began praying for her family. She said she would cry and pray while pressing my brother Clarence's pants! Then, seeing his lack of interest in spiritual things, she once told her sister Alma to direct her prayers toward his younger brother instead: "There's no hope for Clarence. Let's start praying for Joe!"

I grew up wondering why we didn't call her "Aunt Alma," but eventually I realized that my brothers weren't about to call their playmate "Aunt." She was really like a big sister to them, being only a couple of years older than Clarence and Joe. Mom said she would keep track of her boys and Alma swimming in the Severson Dam, by counting heads.

When I was seven, my Father decided to move about 50 miles west into the beautiful Yellowstone Valley, because that was irrigation country. He had gone through several years of drought and crop failure, and had had enough of that. So we moved to a lush town called Fairview, leaving behind my brother Marvin, who stayed so he could finish high school in Watford City.

In those early years, immigrants settled together in neighborhoods and cities, and up until then we had been in a predominantly Scandinavian community. But in the Fairview area where we moved to, most of the people had come from Germany. The state line dividing North Dakota from Montana runs through Fairview, and we used to say that when you drove through town, you had two wheels in North Dakota and two in Montana. From then on I grew up in North Dakota, but most everything I did was in Montana, so I always said I was from Montana. But for Dad, his wheels just went to Montana to shop and he considered himself a North Dakotan.

Although it was only a 50 mile move for us, Fairview seemed very different from Watford City, for it was a beautiful irrigated valley, so different from the dryland we left. What a sight to drive through miles of barren fields and then suddenly look out over an area that was green and vibrant—the Yellowstone Valley. That's where I spent most of my childhood and teenage years.

The farm Dad bought was just four miles from Fairview, and besides the farmland, we had an orchard. During the peak season we picked crab apples, strawberries, choke cherries, and raspberries. There were three long rows of raspberries, and every other day for about three weeks, we picked up to a hundred quarts at a time. Now I can't imagine what we did with all that. Mom canned a lot, and I guess we gave away a lot. Mosquitoes loved the area, so we wore long sleeves. One bush by the road held bull berries. They were red and very bitter, but Aunt Alma loved a bowl of them with milk and sugar when she came to visit.

I remember Mother often saying that when she worked at the restaurant, she had to have three pies baked by breakfast. She was an unusually good cook, and she never just threw things together. I had never seen eggs scrambled with a fork in the frying pan until I was away from home. Mother always whipped up the eggs and then put them in a covered pan over the flame, and they turned out fluffy and tasty.

We had a lot of hens, so we gathered eggs by the dozen. These were put in special boxes and divided into special sections for each egg. At the Valley Cash Store these crates of eggs were exchanged for groceries. I remember us shopping for everything we needed in the food line.

While in high school, my girlfriends and I would sometimes walk to that store at noon and I'd buy a package of cookies or something to munch on, and charge it. I don't ever remember Dad complaining about it or even mentioning it.

Mother canned dozens of quarts of fruit from our orchard, vegetables from the garden, and meat. Her canned beans were out of this world delicious, I thought. Our cellar shelves were full of good food for the cold, winter months. Canning was an art, because if the jars were not sealed properly while the contents were hot, they spoiled, though spoilage was rare.

It took a while for us to be welcomed in Fairview. The kids gave my brother Ray a hard time at school, and me on the walk home. A group of us walked home from school about half a mile to our place, and then the rest walked on to their homes further north. Though I didn't tell her, Mother caught on that the kids were teasing me on the way home, and one afternoon she suddenly appeared, from behind some bushes, and that was the end of that problem. But as the years went by, the girl who was the ringleader became my good friend at school. This was at the Bieber school which had excellent teachers, and one of them eventually decided that Ray should skip seventh grade and I should skip sixth. I've thought through the years that perhaps it wasn't such a smart move, because I feel I missed out on things I should have learned in that grade.

There were three country schools within a four-mile radius, and these all came together to form a two-room school when I was in the eighth grade. A bus picked us up and brought us home and the bus driver was a friendly guy who took turns driving with his wife and son.

Country school programs were a highlight of school days, and parents and family members attended. I remember being up on the platform at a Christmas program when looking way to the back, I spied my brother Joe, who had come home for Christmas. He had his own auto shop in western Montana. Joe could fix anything, and in later years he did extensive factory installation work at Bethany Fellowship in Minnesota. He built a convertible that he drove to New York and took along to India, where he went to do missionary work.

CHAPTER THREE

Family Ties

I knew only one set of grandparents—Mom's parents—who lived 10 miles from us. Dad's parents were in Iowa, and that was like a far-away country in those days. We often went to Watford City to visit Grandma and Grandpa. My Mother's brother, Uncle Ted, lived with them, and he and Grandpa ran the gas station which was next door on the corner. Grandpa was responsible for a church being built nearby. It was Lutheran, but today is Southern Baptist.

I remember that Grandpa prayed with his hands clasped on the table in front of him with his eyes open. He prayed like this both before and after meals. When I was a little girl, I was visiting my grandparents and it was bedtime for a little girl, but I didn't want to go to bed. I remember standing in the stairway watching my Grandfather coming in from outside. He had his hand behind his back. Then he cautiously pulled out a switch which meant if I didn't go to bed I would have a spanking. In a shocked voice I said, "Er duruskute bestefar?" ("Grandpa, are you crazy?") I went to bed right away—I can tell you that! I was just shocked to think that he would think of spanking me!

Grandma was a petite lady, an although she had gone through much heartache in her early married years—losing four children one by one to sickness—she was a cheerful lady who loved to talk. It was all in Norwegian, which she sometimes spoke to my girlfriend Jean, who didn't understand a word of it!

In the Summer, our uncles and their families came home to visit at Grandma and Grandpa's for a couple of weeks. When Uncle Henry and Aunt Helen came from Portland, Jean and I each got a twin to look after, since they brought their boys, James and John. The boys must have been six to eight months old.

Uncle Henry played the guitar and sang. He was a Wesleyan Methodist minister which must have been quite a change for this Lutheran family, which wasn't as conservative doctrinally. I always admired Aunt Helen because she had dark hair and I always believed she looked French. I thought Uncle Henry was wonderful to marry her, and looking back, I thought she was the forerunner to my marrying my husband, Kenny, a dark-haired Assyrian! I heard that there were evangelistic meetings at which Uncle Henry just began to strum his guitar and people began to weep from conviction.

Uncle Joe was a Lutheran Brethren pastor, and he brought his wife Alice home. She was a gifted speaker, too, and I remember her speaking in the high school gym at a meeting. Jesus was everything to her, and just being around her could be convicting. She told of her mother who, once in the middle of baking bread, stopped and washed her hands, and then headed to a neighbor to talk to him about his need of salvation.

God was at work in our family in those early years, drawing us to Himself in various ways and through many different paths.

CHAPTER FOUR

Boys Will Be Boys

When I was a little girl, I was very feminine in spite of having eight brothers. I loved to clean and cook at an early age. The famous Dione Quintuplets were about my age and were all the rage. I remember having them in paper dolls and changes of clothing in paper outfits.

One thing that stands out in my mind was the playhouse I had. There was a new building in our yard that had an empty room, and I turned it into my own little home. I fixed it all up, but there was a clumsy motor in there. I couldn't move it and I didn't want my cozy playhouse destroyed by its presence, so I put a white cloth over it. This brought chuckles from the adults, but that was fine by me. I think of that today and think about how we try to cover something bad with something good, but what we really need to dois move a sin or shortcomings out of our lives—with help if necessary—and not live on trying to keep it covered.

As a child, I had many fears and worries, but we never talked about things like that, so I kept them to myself. As a first grader, I walked to school with my two older brothers, Ernie and Ray. It was a long walk across fields and I was so afraid as we came across bulls grazing along with herds of cattle. I never heard of anyone being attacked by them, but I thought I might be the first one. Then there were groups of cows mooing here and there. The boys told me they could attack people, so I was filled with fear at seeing them, even though my brothers could protect me. My parents had a friend who occasionally came with his wife to visit us and he scared me so much because he said he wanted to take me home with them. Now, I know it was said in friendly fun, but in my little mind, it was a scary thought. Another time I was told that the Salvation Army was coming to town and this thought terrified me because I thought a military invasion was coming! I've often thought how important it is to have children confide in us about their fears, so we can reassure them and further explain things that are troubling them.

I had a lot of headaches as a child, and I now wonder if it wasn't an allergy of some kind. Dad would have me heat my feet in a small tub of warm water and that helped. He took me to a chiropractor when I was about 11, and that was my first encounter with that kind of therapy, which I have been a supporter of all my life.

I was about nine when, after we had just moved to Fairview, my parents were surprised by their earlier friends and neighbors on their silver wedding anniversary. I can still recall looking up and seeing an army of cars full of people coming down that dusty road toward our home. Grandma Aarhus had come over earlier, I suppose to help get ready. Among the guests was Clarence—home from Bible school.

Later, the Fairview News, our faithful community newspaper, noted, "This tells something of the high esteem with which this family was held in their former neighborhood."

As we settled into life in our adopted hometown, we soon had a big surprise in the form of my brother Orvin, who was born when I was nine years old, and my Mother 45! From the very beginning, he was like sunshine in our home. I sometimes used to think to myself, "What would we do if we didn't have Orvin?" He always cheered us up. Everything connected with babies until they were born was so secretive in those days. My Grandma—Mom's Mom—came to visit, and one day she told me in Norwegian that my Mom was going to have a baby, and then she added, "Oh, I guess I shouldn't have told you that!" Mom was surprised that my older brothers enjoyed the new baby so much. There was a 25 year difference between Orvin and my oldest brother Clarence.

Orvin waited for me to come home from school and he knew where the hands on the clock would be when the bus dropped me off. When the older brothers were in the military, Dad gave him geography lessons to teach him where his brothers were serving, and I particularly remember him pointing out Australia on the globe.

Once when Orvin was about two years old, my friend Jean and I were out with him having to cross an irrigation ditch that had a little water in it. We tried to get him across by passing him, but one of us missed the catch and he fell in and only got a little wet.

CHAPTER FIVE

Saved

Standing on the old-fashioned car running board I heard Clarence tell his best friend, Jack, that he had become a Christian. That in itself was a miracle. He was the most unlikely convert of all of us. In those days among Christians, pipe-smoking was frowned upon, but Clarence had five of them. It was a sign of rebellion, and Alma said to me in later years, "Can you imagine Clarence blowing smoke in my face?" I couldn't.

Clarence and Jack went to school together, and also played banjos, but at that point, their lives took opposite turns. Clarence was teaching in a country school, but decided to quit and go to Minnesota to attend Bible school. He later told me that he didn't dare tell Dad what he was doing. He would come home for vacations in the summer, and was a great encouragement to Mom, I knew, because he reinforced her faith and commitment to God, something my father hadn't been supportive of. Clarence played his guitar and sang. I particularly remember him singing "The Meeting in the Air."

When I was 11, I went to Watford City to attend evangelistic meetings held by my two uncles, Joe and Henry, along with Clarence, at the high school gymnasium. I stayed at my Grandparents' house and this was also about the time I met Jean Bond, who became my lifelong friend. Her family members were friends of my mom's brother, Uncle Tommy, and Aunt Edna.

Two singers from Clarence's Bible school came to do the music. I was very touched and the Holy Spirit began a work in my heart during these meetings. After one service, I was already outside, but I left Jean and rushed back in. I found one of the singers, Bernice Nelson, and told her I wanted to be saved. I was crying. She led me in prayer and I asked Jesus to come into my heart that night.

When Clarence put me on the train to go back home to Fairview, he gave me a New Testament and said, "Don't forget to tell Dad." One day I woke up after having fallen asleep reading my little New Testament, and found Dad sitting beside me leafing through it. What a good opportunity it would have been to have told him, but I wasn't brave enough. I often thought what would have happened if I had given him a clear testimony of what Jesus had done for me, but I was afraid to, and never had the courage to tell him. It was a full six years before he would make a decision for himself.

Mother told me later that she noticed a change in me after I came home after being saved. I was singing around the house and she hoped it would last. Outwardly I got lost in the shuffle of life around me, but inwardly I knew I was saved, although I wasn't ready to give myself completely to the Lord. Somehow I thought I'd never have fun any more, that life would be boring if I fully surrendered to Christ. What a mistaken notion that was.

I went to confirmation classes every Saturday afternoon with a bunch of other kids, and this was very good for me as we had to memorize a lot of Scripture. After two years we were confirmed. This included a grilling about the Catechism and the Bible before the church, and then a confirmation ceremony and communion. It meant a lot to me and I took it all seriously. We went to Williston and Mom and Dad bought me a new suit and dress for the ceremony. These were classy outfits. The name of the store was Joseph's—a name I would become very familiar with in the years ahead.

A new fellow, Nick, had moved with his parents into our community and I was interested in him, and he in me! He also went to confirmation classes each Saturday, so one day he came by just as we were eating, and asked my Dad, "Is Lila ready to go and confess her sins?" My Dad wasn't about to let his girl go with him, and he maintained that firm stand for my entire teen years. My Dad may not have been a Christian, but he had high moral standards, and was very protective of me, his only daughter. Later, when Nick went into the Navy, he wrote me two postcards, so I wrote him back two letters. Lloyd chased me all around the yard to get to see those postcards. We always got a lot of mail, and one day Dad brought the mail home, and he was looking through it cradled in his left arm. I was right at his side checking while holding my breath! All of a sudden I saw my two letters—they had been returned because Nick had moved. Dad said nonchalantly, "I wonder why his mail is coming here." Years later I wrote him, "Dad, you couldn't help but see your little girl's name and address in the corner of that envelope, but you didn't say a word!" He probably sensed the agony I was going through, and left it at that! When I was in my first year of college, I got a blue Valentine box of candy from Nick. But then he married someone else, so that was the end of that.

Though I wasn't old enough to get a driver's license, I was about 14 when I had my brother Lloyd's car and took some of my friends out for a ride. These were country roads without much traffic. Coming around a bend, I didn't quite make it, and the front right wheel veered off the road. There we sat, probably wondering how we could get back on the road, when suddenly I saw a man working in a field right near us. However, my hopes of getting help without getting in trouble were dashed when I saw that it was a friend of Lloyd's. He came and helped us get back on the road, but I knew it was just a matter of time until he told Lloyd, and then I'd be in trouble.

A few days later, I walked into the kitchen where he and Mom were talking, and he said, "The tie rod in my car is bent." "Here we go," I thought but didn't say a word. Then he added, "Lila, do you know anything about that?" So I had to 'fess up, but that was the end of it. My worrying was for naught.

CHAPTER SIX

But For The Grace Of God...

During my junior year in high school, I went to live with my friend, Jean Bond, and her family, and attended school in Watford with her. She was a senior, and I had no Christian friends where we lived, and was gradually being pulled by the glamour and temptations of the world in our small town. Living with Jean's family I was being discipled, whether I wanted to be or not. They were strong Christians and went to a Bible Presbyterian Church, so I always went with them to Sunday school, church, and young people's meetings. I don't remember exactly why this all came about, but I have a sneaking suspicion that my father may have engineered it to keep me away from some boys in my hometown that he thought were up to no good.

Later it seemed so strange to me that I had been 50 miles away from my parents, whom I loved so much, for an entire year, but I also came to the realization that this was God's way of protecting me. Dad paid $20 a month to the Bond family for me to stay with them that year.

One thing Jean and I were good at was laughing. We would laugh easily and hard at a lot of things. I don't think that one Sunday school teacher thought we would amount to much the way we could cut up. Once Alma told us that we should ask ourselves, "Is it kind, is it necessary, and is it true?" before we said something about anyone. That put us in a bind, so once as we were sitting in the car watching people go by on the street, if we thought there was something funny about them, we didn't say anything, but we just looked at each other and laughed. We had kept the letter of that law! Alma gave each of us a pair of little wooden shoes attached to a cloth pendant to wear on a blouse or shirt. The shoes had "Jean" on one and "Lila" on the other. I have both sets hanging up by my kitchen, since Jean's daughter, Mary, sent hers to me after Jean went to Heaven.

Jean's parents kept a tight reign on us, and we had to live up to high standards. We also went to Youth for Christ meetings on Saturday nights where I played the guitar and we sang duets. Sometimes in the evenings we sat on their porch and sang and someone once scolded us. We were probably singing something like, "...send us a letter; send it by mail, send it in care of Birmingham Jail." Jean's Mom didn't like another song we sang, and now that I have children and grandchildren, I understand why. It was about a little boy who had been scolded and pleaded, "Don't make me go to bed and I'll be good." It was a sad song because he died in the night.

On Saturday nights, the youth from our church would go roller skating in another town 12 miles away. We got paired off with Christian boys, and even though I really didn't like the boy I often went with, it was a way to get to the roller skating rink! Jean ended up marrying her then-date, but I didn't like mine and I would come home and confide my feelings about him to Jean's sister, Edith, who also lived with us. I considered her a "safe" confidant, since her boyfriend was overseas and she was devoted to him. I was quite vocal in my dislike for this young man before cutting off relations completely. I'd come home from skating and tell her what I didn't like about him. He was very handsome with a nice smile, but now I realize God didn't want me settling down there and had other plans for me.

Imagine my shock and embarrassment when some years later Edith broke up with the soldier and married the guy I would gripe to her about! It took us a while to get over that, but we did and all became good friends.

Edith worked in the town drug store, and since hosiery was hard to get during World War II, she had first dibs and helped us get some pairs. The drugstore carried more than just drugs, and there was a glass counter with jewelry. I loved a heart necklace and would sometimes admire it. One day to my sadness, it was gone. But what a surprise when I got it for my birthday! Edith told Dad about my liking it and he had bought it for me.

When it came time for my senior year, I went back to Fairview High school, and my seatmate was a good Christian Nazarene girl who also became Valedictorian of our class. So again, even though I wasn't very happy about it, I was stuck because God brought more godly influences into my life that kept me from wandering too far away from Him.

When Clarence pastored a church in Superior, Wisconsin, he fell in love with his pianist, a young woman named Jeanette Nelson. They decided to get married in Wisconsin and came home to us for a visit. Finally I had a sister! We loved her so much right from the beginning. Then he was sent to Japan to serve as a chaplain with the U.S. military and she went to Bible school in Minneapolis. Between my junior and senior years, she came out to visit and she, Alma, and I once took a trip to Seattle. It was fun to be with them, but I remember we visited Lake Sammamish Bible Camp, and I was very uncomfortable because I wasn't ready to give myself wholeheartedly to the Lord. Conviction was what it was. So while they went to prayer meetings, I pretended to be asleep. When our visit was over, we left Alma in Seattle, and Jeanette and I returned home. We visited relatives and I had my first roller-coaster ride. I thought if I ever got out of that alive, I'd never go again. But I changed my mind and went again right away.

I enjoyed my senior year of high school the most, because I could take subjects I liked. Typing II, Shorthand II, English, Journalism, and History were my favorites. My English teacher was Lloyd's high school classmate, and her parents had a drugstore. She made Macbeth and other classics easy to understand. We had a school paper which the Journalism class put out, and I remember one story I wrote for it entitled, "Johnny Got a Zero Today." Johnny was not a good student when he was in school, but when he hit an enemy plane (a Zero) he was a hero. Writing for that paper was my first foray into journalism.

When my brother Joe came home on military furlough once, he talked Ray into going with him someplace. I'll never forget the morning Ray came home while Joe went on to his military station. My bedroom was just off the kitchen, and I heard Ray tell Mom he had gotten saved! I'm sorry to admit that I thought, "Oh brother, he'll never be any fun anymore!" He was always joking and the life of any event. Mom told him to tell Dad. He said he had on the way home in the car, and Dad had said, "I'm going with you." That was one of the first steps of showing spiritual interest on my Dad's part.

I always remember coming home from school and talking a lot with Mom. She listened and was a good sounding board for me during high school. Of course, I know I only told her what I knew wouldn't upset her. Wearing lipstick was absolutely forbidden, so I got by that by putting it on after I left the house.

During my Senior year there were to be contests somewhere in Montana for typing and shorthand students, and my teacher wanted me to compete. I had once typed on our manual typewriters for 10 minutes at 69 words a minute with no errors, and she put that paper on the bulletin board. I should add that when I first started to take typing, one day the teacher said, "Lila, if you don't memorize your keyboard, I'm going to take the board down." In those days there were no letters on the typewriter itself, just a big keyboard on the wall in the front of the room up high. So we kept looking at that until we memorized it.

I also liked shorthand and had gotten awards, so my teacher was anxious for me to go to the state competition. But around that time Joe came for a visit and wanted Ray and me to go with him to a spring conference at Prairie Bible Institute, across the border in Canada. I wasn't all that keen on it, but Ray, Alma, and I ended up going with him. The trip would take us across most of Montana before crossing into Canada.

On that trip, all of us almost went to heaven, too. Joe was driving, Ray was beside him, and Alma and I were in back. I distinctly remember leaning forward to see how fast he was going and it was 62 miles an hour, driving across the opens plans of Montana. Suddenly he was having trouble. The steering wheel was spinning in circles, and we sailed off the road between fence posts and out into a field before coming to a stop. Alma, from the back seat, was gasping, "It's OK Joe, it's OK!" Later she wondered what in the world she meant because it certainly was not OK. Once Joe, the mechanically-minded one, managed to find a temporary fix for the tie-rod, we resumed driving. Later, we saw numerous places where, had we gone off, we would not have lived to tell the story. At the next town, we got the car fully fixed. We have always marveled at that incident because within ten years all of us in that car were spread across the globe as missionaries: Joe in India, Ray in Africa, Alma on Taiwan, and me in Japan.

I was not impressed with Prairie, because for one thing, you couldn't play baseball, or anything, really, with the boys. They had strict dress codes, and the dresses were long. A girl visiting from Seattle was going around saying she was coming back in the fall for school, and I was thinking, "You'll never catch me here!" She never did attend, but I did, that fall.

When I got back to high school from our trip to Canada, my girlfriend told me that the principal and my typing and shorthand teacher had been discussing my absence. But I didn't hear anything except my teacher lamenting, "Lila, you missed last week's contest." That, too, I felt later, was of the Lord, because I was not derailed from what God wanted me to do when I finished high school: to go to Prairie and train to become a missionary.

But I didn't know my destiny at that point, and really didn't know what I wanted to do after High School. I wrote to a nursing school in Minot, from which my sister-in-law, Myrtle, later graduated, asking about nursing. But then my parents said they wanted me to have one year of Bible school and then I could go into nursing. It was a decision that would set the course for the rest of my life.

CHAPTER SEVEN

War

My high school years were filled with war—World War II, to be exact—and as a family with a half dozen young men ripe for military service, we were deeply affected. Everyone was very patriotic and my teen years meant seeing five of my brothers head off to serve.

Marvin was drafted first. He had attended Billings Business College so it was only natural that he became company clerk in his unit. Once he confided to Dad that with that job he couldn't advance beyond the rank of corporal. Dad encouraged him to stay where he was because it was safer than being in direct combat. However, we learned later that he was once miraculously spared when his unit was marching across a bridge in Germany where he served with General Patton's famed Third Infantry Division. Marvin, exhausted, fell asleep walking and the soldier behind him kept him from falling over the bridge they were crossing.

Clarence, who was a Pastor in Wisconsin, was next to enlist, serving as a chaplain after theological training at Harvard. He was then sent to Japan. Once he sent our parents a telegram that read, "It's twins, but it doesn't make you grandparents." He had been promoted to second lieutenant, so he got two bars on his shoulder.

Then Joe, who had attended the State School of Science at Wapheton, North Dakota, and at one time had his own car maintenance business in Western Montana, decided to go to Prairie. After about two years, he came home for a visit and was promptly drafted into the Army. There he was assigned to a dog training unit. Once he sent a big dog home to our folks, and Dad went to the train station to pick him up and bring him home. His name was Fritz, and he came complete with official papers and tags around his neck.

Next, Norman was drafted and sent to the Philippines. We didn't hear from him for quite a while, and when we asked him about that after he came home, he said with a wry smile that he had been "in a hot spot." Later, he was hit by shrapnel and flown back to the States and was awarded the Purple Heart, the symbol of bravery in combat. The boys didn't talk much about their wartime experiences, and he was no exception.

I still remember when Lloyd left. He had enlisted in the Navy and left one afternoon—a sad day for me. He was a great tease and a lot of fun. Hawaii was his eventual destination.

Ernie was called up, but he didn't pass the medical exam. Mom said that had he been drafted, she would have complained to the draft board. We think the board probably said "hey, five from one family is enough!" Still, it was a great disappointment to Ernie to not be able to join his brothers in fighting for his country.

When my heroic brothers came home on leave, they always came to church with us and the pastor, Rev. Peterson, never failed to publicly recognize and welcome them. A flag with a red star for each serviceman from the church hung in the front of the building. We were so proud of them in their crisp uniforms. It was great to welcome them, but hard to see them leave when their furloughs ended. I felt sad for Mom and Dad, who tried to be so brave. I was glad when they left at night because we could sleep on it and feel better in the morning, but if they left in the morning I felt sad all day. Usually, before they were sent overseas, they had a furlough, so we never knew if we would see them again. But these things were never discussed out loud and even though we didn't discuss painful things like that, we had ways of dealing with our difficulties, especially using humor. We used to hear a joke about the little boy who asked his mom what the gold stars stood for, and she stated they were "for men who died in the service." To which he asked, "Was it the morning service or the evening service?"

Mom was home alone the day word of Norman's accident came. The postman came to our home and handed her a telegram from the State Department and expressed the condolences of the community. After he left, Mom opened it and it read: "We regret to inform you that your son, PFC Norman Finsaas, has been slightly wounded in action..." but in her haste, she read seriously instead of slightly. All day long she lived with the thought that he was near death. When Dad came home that night he asked if there was any mail and she told him there was a telegram on the table. He read it and said, "Well, it could have been worse." She said, "what do you mean?" He answered that it said slightly wounded.

Through bombings and nightmarish fighting; through travel by air; sea and land; my five brothers were kept safe and all returned safely after World War II. I feel now that it was because of something called "Joe's Petition."

The envelope was old and brownish. It appeared to have been around for a long time, probably handled a lot. I found it in an old family album and realized that it was over 70 years old. On the outside in my late Mother's handwriting, I read, "Joe's Petition." Inside that envelope was a single sheet of paper—so seemingly insignificant, but as I unfolded it and looked at it, I was flooded with memories: sad ones, happy ones, and thankful ones. I soon realized that our family's destiny had been greatly determined by what I was looking at. I learned something valuable about the past, and a lesson for now—for myself, and to pass on to others, from that one little sheet of paper that read:

"There are now five of us boys in the service. One overseas. We don't know how soon the rest of us may be on our way across, or how soon one or two of the boys at home will have to go. The Lord has said, Matt. 18:19 "that if two of you shall agree on earth about anything that they shall ask, it shall be done for them of my Father which is in heaven." I believe it would please the Lord if we join together and claim this promise...protection and safe return of each...but above all, Christ's purpose be accomplished in the lives of each of us. May we acknowledge our approval, acceptance with our signatures."
–**Mr. J. Aarhus, Mrs. Aarhus, Theodore Aarhus, Henry B. Aarhus, Helen M. Aarhus, Joseph Aarhus, Alma Aarhus, Alice Aarhus, Mother, Dad, Raymond Finsaas, Lila Finsaas**

Years later we learned that Alma had had a dream around this time. She saw five airplanes go out, but only four return back. I can only imagine how she prayed and her relief when the last "airplane"—the chaplain from Japan—came home. I believe that their safe returns were because of "Joe's Petition."

Looking back, I can see that God fully answered that petition—not only by bringing each back, but by accomplishing His purposes in each of their lives. Ray and I were profoundly influenced by the lives of our returned brothers, with two of them guiding us into ministry. This eventually led Ray to become a missionary to Africa, and me to Japan. The chaplain, Clarence, resumed his pastorate. Joe spent many years in missionary work in India and Nepal.

Blessings have continued on the next generation, producing talented nurses, teachers, farmers, businessmen, musicians, house wives, missionaries, film producers, writers, and even an airplane pilot! What would happen if families made pacts like this? Grandparents, aunts and uncles, cousins, children, and grandchildren verbalizing their faith in, and claim of, God's mighty promises? Why not try it? Surely we would see greater family unity and blessing if we had more "Joe's Petitions."

CHAPTER EIGHT

From Prairie to Prairie

It was late summer when Mom and Dad deputized Clarence, who was home for a short visit, to talk to me about going to Prairie as we sat on the back lawn. I loved him a lot and they knew he had a way with me. But I was stubborn. He said later that he almost gave up. He talked about my attending Prairie and I said, "Why can't I go to the school you went to?" He replied, "Well, because Mom and Dad want you to go to Prairie." I felt that I could have bluffed my way through most other schools, but instinctively I knew I couldn't at Prairie. He asked me why I disliked it so much. I said, "Well, those long skirts the girls have to wear!" He countered so sensibly, "Did you ever think that if everyone has long ones and you have a short one on, you'd feel funny and out of place?"

I hadn't thought of it that way, but it made sense. So I agreed to go, and they said "just one year," then I could go into nurses' training. Grandma Aarhus took me aside and gave me a special hug before I left at 17. It was like she knew that we'd never be together again on this earth because she passed away a few months later. Mom wrote that her funeral was like a coronation, with several pastors taking part.

Joe, Ray, and I went by train, which took us halfway across Montana before we could cross the border. We stayed overnight in Calgary, about 90 miles from Three Hills, in the Alberta area of Canada, taking a bus the next day. I had a closet full of clothes at home, but could only take the tops, as all my skirts were just at the knee. Mom hurriedly made me four skirts: a black, grey, red patterned plaid, and brown one. I put one on before we left Calgary and rolled it up at the waist about four times, letting it down when we got to Three Hills. Interestingly, the next year long skirts were back in fashion, and Mr. Maxwell, the head of Prairie quipped to the students, "The world tells you to put 'em down and you do. When the school does, it's a problem!"

Prairie began a new and exciting era for me. I loved living in the dorm and had lots of friends. I'd write home about my roommates Mary, Sally, Dorie, Kats (Kathleen), Myrt, Esther, Ella, and Hildred…so that I think Mom and Dad almost felt they knew them before they ever met them.

We had arrived at Prairie a little late, so when I went to my first homiletics class, the professor announced that there would be an exam next time on the material covered so far. I knew I had a good excuse, so I got the notes from a girl in class and copied them. It took me all study hour that evening just to copy them. When I returned her notes and was walking down the hall, it came very clearly to me: "Take that test." I had never experienced anything like this, and it was just like a matter-of-fact thing. So the next day I took the exam with everyone else and to my shock, I got 100%. That was an incident that reminded me that God was well able to make up to me what I needed if I obeyed Him. I did learn how to study, however, since I had not learned that in high school and I remember flunking only one exam in all four years, getting a 69%, and that was one on the references of Bible verses.

Soon it was time for the annual Fall Conference, and classes stopped, so we could go to the sessions. Dr. Armin Gesswein, from

Seattle, was the main speaker, and he spoke on the topic, "Have you received the Holy Spirit since you believed?" from the book of Acts. One night he had us pray and ask to be filled with the Holy Spirit. I knew I was saved, but I was still a rebel. But I did pray seriously and lots of other people evidently did, too, because revival broke out and continued for several days. Students lined up at the microphones to confess sin and ask for forgiveness. Mr. Maxwell handled it all very wisely, however, and managed it well. For instance, when guys would confess that they had been "flirting" he put a stop to that. Revival needs wise guidance and leadership or they can go off the deep end. In my lifetime this was the first and only time I had been privileged to see and take part in revival firsthand. It was an awesome, life-changing experience.

Here's how one classmate remembered Rev. Gesswein's speech:

> *Sharing his experiences from the great awakening in Norway, he taught us that true revival includes repentance—Christians getting right with God and with one another. During one of the afternoon meetings, a missionary from China got up to give a report of his work. He stood with bowed head for some time, then looked up and said, "I was planning to give you a glowing report of my ministry. But in all honesty, I can't." His voice shook with emotion. All I can say is that I've been a miserable failure on the mission field," he said as tears filled his eyes. "Pray for me." The missionary sat down and buried his face in his hands. His shoulders shook with sobs. We were thunderstruck. A long silence followed. Gradually, we became aware that we were in the presence of a holy God who will not tolerate sin. I remember one handsome young man in the balcony who rose and said with a broken voice, "I've led some of you to believe that I lived a victorious life in the army, but I did not. I failed the Lord many times. I ask you to forgive me." Like a field of grain bending in a gale, the whole auditorium of people bowed low before a holy God. The wind of His Spirit penetrated every recess of our hearts, convicting us of hidden*

sins—some long forgotten. All we could do was cry, "Oh, God, have mercy! Oh God, forgive me. Cleanse me." Tears flowed. Sin became "exceedingly sinful." One person after another arose to confess sin in trembling voice. Since we had difficulty hearing them in the large auditorium, Mr. Maxwell suggested that they come to the platform and use the microphone. Soon a long line formed across the front and down the full length of the building. The rest remained in prayer. We were all so conscious of the presence of God that we cared nothing about people's opinions. All we wanted to do was to get rid of the awful burden of sin weighing heavily upon us. The meeting went on hour after hour. We were oblivious of time. Supper time came and went. The cooks were told to hold the meal until later. Still the people stood in line–young and old, students and staff–awaiting their opportunity to confess sin before God and man. Late that night, the principal reluctantly dismissed the meeting and said we could have dinner if we wanted to. Most of us did not. We were too overcome with the presence of a holy God and the awfulness of our sins to care about food or sleep. The next morning the meeting took up where it left off the night before. As I recall, there was not much preaching that day. Just another long line of people wanting to confess their sins. More weeping. More praying. The holy hush of God was upon the place. It was an awesome spectacle. Some confession was done privately. Students went to teachers to confess cheating or a bad attitude. Others apologized to friends for a lack of love or for criticism. Letters of apology were written. Money owed was paid back. Borrowed books were returned. No sin seemed too small. Pride was just as heinous as stealing. Gossip was as wretched as immorality. As time went on, we felt like onions being peeled. We got rid of one sin and there was yet another. I'm not sure how long this went on, perhaps for three or four days. We asked the Holy Spirit then to fill us as clean, empty vessels. Oh, the joy that flooded in! We almost skipped around campus. From that group of revived students, a great army later went to the mission fields of the world to share the Good News."

I remember waking up in the mornings after that filled with unusual peace and joy, and thinking, "I thought if I really gave myself to the Lord I wouldn't be happy or have any fun anymore." I knew I had believed the enemy's lies. It was the beginning of a wonderful life living close to the Lord Jesus.

But I also had restitution to make. I'm so glad I was only 17 so I hadn't had time enough to be too wicked! I do remember after that thinking that I wasn't doing anything I was afraid my parents would find out about, but I did have to write some letters asking for forgiveness, even one to my parents. I remember Mom writing how happy she was for me and that she hoped it would last. I also wrote to my high school principal asking for forgiveness for cheating on exams. Had I known that he was so touched that he read the letter to the whole school, I might not have wanted to go back home when school was out! He got a similar letter from another student, I learned, and he wrote me back with forgiveness for anything I remembered.

From then on most of the rules didn't bother me and we joked about the ones that did. The classes were hard, but I also studied hard and learned a lot, since I felt I had a lot to learn. We had a lot of fun in the dorms and got to know kids from all over, but rules were strict, though. Study hours started at 7:30 pm, lights were out at 10, and on again at six in the morning. Once the girls across the hall were noisy after study hours started so I wrote them a note and told them to appear at the Dean's office on Saturday morning and signed the name of the girl in charge of our hall. My roommate and I were watching their door and listening and she said, "They know you wrote it."

We went back to our studies and I just forgot the whole thing, that is until Saturday morning as we were heading out to play basketball in the gym. There I met those two girls coming out of the Dean's office. I was shocked and blurted out, "Where have you been?" They replied that it was none of my business, but then told me the story and I said that I wrote the note. They said they'd go back and explain and a few days later I had to see the dean for something. She was formidable–an older lady who was totally in charge and firm. "Lila, I've been waiting for you to come and see me. This could be a demerit!" she said. The problem was my signing someone else's name, she explained. I never did get the demerit though, and she kept in touch with us in Japan until she passed away.

In college, I did go through a period of subtle condemnation, however, in high school. I didn't have a conscience that bothered me much–like the time I skipped school and went with a friend and made cream puffs, and I wrote my own excuse and signed Mom's name–but now I felt guilty about too many things. Did I do that right? Was I honest in what I said? My roommate seemed to sense this and one day I came across this verse and read it to her: "There is therefore now no condemnation to those who are in Christ Jesus..." and Esther strongly blurted out, "Now take it, then!" I learned that I John 1:9 is in the Bible and it has meant so much to me through the years: "If we confess our sins, He is faithful and just to forgive us our sins, and to cleanse us from all unrighteousness."

The first year slipped by, and in April the annual Spring Conference was held. Mom, Dad, Alma, and Orvin came up to attend that and to take us home. Radio preacher Charles E. Fuller of the Old Fashioned Revival Hour was one of the main speakers and at one session Dad and Orvin were saved. That was so special. They teased me on the return trip about something waiting at home. I was to guess what it was. It was cold and it was hot, it was white and it was black. Turned out that electricity had come into the neighborhood during that year and we had our first refrigerator and stove.

At home that summer I taught Vacation Bible School in Nohly, Montana. When I asked the kids to bring a Bible from home, one boy said they only had a "Holy Bible," and he wondered if it would be ok if he brought that. The next year I heard that a young seminary student was sent to teach this group, and when he talked to them about being saved by baptism, one of the boys asked, "Don't you have to be born again?" He supposedly answered, "I know where you got that!" Hopefully, eternity will reveal some who were born again during our VBS days.

During my teen years, we had become close friends with some people who lived in Nohly. They were from the same denomination as my parents, but were also being fed spiritually by radio preachers like Charles E. Fuller and Theodore H. Epp of the Back to the Bible broadcast, and a local program featuring Rev. and Mrs. Hoff. Mom and the ladies were good friends, and exchanged thoughts whenever we could get together, which wasn't all that often. Margaret Borg in Sidney was one, and another was Tillie Storvik and her daughter.

That summer I was also asked to help at a Bible camp near Bloomfield, Montana and a pastor and his wife came and got me. After I left, Dad got really worried about me because they didn't know the people who came for me, anything about the camp, or even where it was. I wasn't aware of any of this, but Norman and Marvin came to the camp to check it out. I'm sure I was happy to see them and didn't realize the reason they had come.

We had a great time at camp and there were great speakers, and the directors were a wonderful couple. After I got home, I turned on the radio to listen to Rev. and Mrs. Hoff's daily program, who were also guests. That made me lonesome for camp.

Then there were three more years at Prairie, and I always came home for the summers. I met a girl at school named Myrtle Dahl, who came to visit me one summer. We taught together at a Vacation Bible School, which was held in a desolate, hilly area across the river from Sidney, Montana. We stayed in a teacher's quarters and taught in the public schoolhouse. One night we were petrified as we heard some howling outside. There were no telephones and we were stranded. When we went home during a break, Dad said he had heard there was a mountain lion in the area and he wasn't happy that we were in this dangerous place, but I couldn't see how a mountain lion could have gotten into the teacher's quarters. We taught at various places in Montana, as well and Ray and Marj Ruth, some close friends, remember us coming home and finding us sitting on their porch, waiting.

Sometime during my senior year at Prairie, I began to have a serious struggle because I was feeling that God wanted me to be a missionary. My idea of a missionary wasn't very favorable. I remember telling Mom once, as a teenager, that one thing I never wanted to be was a missionary. I had never met one so I had nothing to go on. She countered by wondering why I felt like that. I told her plainly that I felt they were people who "couldn't get any other job." She said, "Well, I feel just the opposite. They have to be able to do so many things!" Interestingly, later on I visited one of my elementary school teachers and she said she remembered my telling her that I wanted to be "a mommy and a missionary."

During this time of inner struggle I remembered having heard someone say that if there's something God is asking you to do and you just can't, pray that you are "willing to be made willing." So since the thought of leaving my parents and going to a strange country seemed so outlandish, I decided to do that. Before I was fully aware of it, my rebellion was gone and I was very interested in becoming a missionary.

During one of my years at Prairie, Clarence and Jeanette came for the Spring Conference, introducing me to two missionaries from Japan—Anne Dievendorf and her sister, Mabel Frances. They were rather famous and had stayed in Japan during the war, even having to be on their own at one point, as their mission board wanted them to leave.

Japan seemed to be the place God wanted me, and so I went to a Japan prayer meeting at the room of a Japanese girl attending Prairie. She later came to Japan herself and served for many years.

Studying occupied much of my time, but as a senior I taught a Sunday school class of fellow classmates. We met once during each week to go over the lesson under the tutelage of a lady named

Mrs. Waldock whose husband was on the staff in the office. Choir was also something I enjoyed, and the director, Mrs. Tygert, was an outstanding soloist. Just before she and her husband left for Japan as missionaries, she sang a solo at a Sunday morning service, but broke down and couldn't finish.

I always loved the piano, and here was my chance to take lessons. One year I enjoyed this, but the second year I had a teacher who scared me so I dropped out for a whole year. Then wisdom got to me and I decided I was not going to let one teacher keep me from something I loved. So my senior year I applied for piano lessons again and this time my teacher was a young senior student, Vivian, who became a lifelong friend and later served with her husband and family in Japan, living not far from us for a while. Vivian not only made the piano come alive, but she encouraged me and taught me things like doing runs. She was creative. But I had a problem in that if I could just hear a song once, I could play it, so that kept me from digging into figuring out the notes, which I find difficult even today. If I had only known that a lady who sang and played the piano for herself over our local Sidney, Montana, radio station couldn't read a note, I would have felt encouraged. I've heard that she started taking lessons, but ended up in tears because it was easier for her to play by ear. How we loved to listen to her on Sunday afternoons on the radio! I've had to play the piano most of my missionary years, and

I enjoy it.

CHAPTER NINE

"You'll Never Make a Missionary!"

As a senior at Prairie, I wrote to a missionary sending agency called TEAM about mission work in Japan. They told me I was too young and needed either more schooling or training. So, I decided to go to Grand Rapids, Minnesota, and helped Clarence and Jeanette in their church for the next year. This was a great experience, and I taught junior high kids who almost overflowed our little room in the church. I also taught junior high kids at Vacation Bible School over the summer.

> *Our family lived in northern Minnesota and we attended a church where Lila's brother Clarence was the pastor. During that summer, Lila was visiting and volunteered to teach Vacation Bible School. I was deeply touched by her teaching and strong faith. I later learned that she went on to be a missionary in Japan and that two of her brothers were also missionaries. When I finished college and seminary and got married, my wife and I spent 30 years in Africa as missionaries. Part of my calling, I believe, goes back to those formative years and my path crossing with Lila so many years ago.*
>
> **- Rodney Venberg**

It was fun living with them and their kids, Sharon, Renee and Barbara and Jeanette's mother, Mrs. Nelson. I also went with Clarence and played the piano when he ministered at a senior citizen's home and we sang duets most every Sunday. Jeanette was the pianist, and he always introduced me with "my sister will now join me in a duet."

During this time I worked for an attorney named, John J. Benton. This was a new experience but I enjoyed it and learned a lot. I put all my secretarial training to good use as there were no computers, so he dictated letters and legal forms and I typed them out. I also went through all the files and arranged them with new labels. Mr. Benton was very kind to me and I had my own knotty pine office next to his. Before that I worked for three weeks at another legal office that was old and so smoke-smelling that I reeked when I left it.... to go and visit homes for the church.

At Christmas time, Mr. Benton found out that I hadn't been home for the holidays for four years while I was away at Prairie, so he gave me time off to go home. Joe was at Bethany, and he had bought a new car for Dad, so we drove it home.

Back at work, the time was drawing near for me to move on and go home for the summer. Mr. Benton knew I was not there permanently and he really wanted me to stay. One day he came into my office, sat on the couch by the opposite wall, and said, "What don't you like about this place?" I asked him if he really wanted me to tell him. He said he did and I replied that I didn't like the profanity, because between the lawyers and their clients there was plenty of that. He quipped, "Well, there hasn't been much since you came!" Then he added, "You'll never make a missionary!" I asked him why and he said, "Because you're too happy. They always look like they've lost their best friend!"

CHAPTER TEN

Chicago

After a summer at home the Evangelical Alliance Mission (TEAM) invited me to work in their Chicago office. Ray was also a missionary candidate, so he came as well. We had separate apartments, but shared a kitchen. He worked downtown for some months, and then headed back home to get ready for his upcoming wedding to Myrtle.

This was also a great experience, both with roommates and colleagues in the office. My jobs were varied, as they put us candidates wherever there was a need. For a while I worked at the switchboard on Saturdays, and had Mondays off. Learning this job gave me a nervous stomach for the first time in my life because calls came in from all over and I had to take the messages or switch them to the right people. When I got used to it, the busier it was, the better. One Saturday, my boss, Dr. Mortenson, called in from his home and dictated about 20 letters on the phone which I then typed up as Saturday wasn't very busy at the switchboard.

I remembered that challenging and stomach churning experience when a short time later I went to a meeting in Montana where a man said, "The Lord told me that there is a lady coming in here that has trouble with her stomach, and if she comes forward, we'll pray for her."

It was just a small meeting at a church or home with about ten people there. When no one responded to his call, he and his wife who were conducting these meetings, dismissed the meeting. I thought long and hard about what he had said and how God had given me a chance to be healed, and I was just too proud to go up there and receive it. So I went up to him and asked him, "Do you think you were talking about me?" He said, "Yes I was, but I didn't want to embarrass you." He and his wife prayed for me and God did heal me.

A lot of us went to an Evangelical Free church nearby, where the pastor was a former missionary to Africa. Singing in the choir was special, and we had practice once a week with an outstanding director and his wife. One of my roommates was Baptist, but she didn't like to go alone to that church, so she grudgingly went with me. One day she griped, "I know why it's called the Free church, because you can believe anything you want to!" I was very proud of Ray for giving her a little history lesson on the beginnings of the Free church, even though that wasn't his background, either.

The time came for Ray to go home and after he left, I found an envelope on the table with his writing on it. I remember turning it over because I got lonesome for him, just looking at his handwriting. In April, I took time off to go home to be in his wedding. They were going to have as their wedding motto, "United to Serve in Japan," but decided instead on just "United to Serve," which proved to be wise because they ended up in Africa, where they spent many fruitful and faithful years.

Working in the TEAM office in Chicago meant meeting many godly people, both men and women, old and young, on a daily basis from all over the world. We had devotions each morning in a downstairs room and sat in a big circle, some 20 of us. One day the founder of TEAM, an old African missionary, Dr. T.J. Bach, got up and went somewhere and then came back and sat down. When the director questioned him on it he said nonchalantly, "I just went to give Brother Swanson a hug." Such love permeated the headquarters.

For a time I worked in the filing department, which proved to be training that I've used all my life in Japan. We had to be able to find letters and records as far as seven years back, and if it was more than a few years back, we had to go to a basement where old records were kept. Most of the mail from all departments ended up on my desk, and that was most interesting. Once I asked Goldye, the boss's secretary, if he never wrote a mean or caustic letter. She said she had known him to write them, but he put them in his desk and then later ended up throwing them away. That's why I never saw any, and had such respect for him and for all the rest of the staff and workers.

During this time, Candidate School—a two week intensive course—was held at Trinity Seminary for missionary candidates. I attended it along with 25 others. Several of us ended up in Japan; others went to different countries.

One highlight of my time in Chicago was getting to know Clara Anderson, who was a colon therapist and nutritionist. She lived in Wheaton, and some of us would go out there to be with her and learn from her and have treatments.

Clara's daughter and son-in-law were missionaries in Japan at the time, under a Baptist mission. She rented out rooms in her big house, and was like a mother to many of us. Sometime after I left, I heard that she took a trip to Norway and at that time on the plane she prayed something like, "Lord, things are going too good for me; bring something hard into my life." That was not a smart prayer, as she learned later, as tragedy upon tragedy came upon her once tranquil life. It wasn't long after that prayer that her daughter suffered a nervous breakdown in Japan. The family was forced to return to the States, and eventually a divorce ensued.

A Chinese missionary friend of ours named William Schubert once said he wouldn't even sing the verse of the well known hymn that says, "Let sorrow do its work; bring grief or pain," because he said his wife died in China, leaving him with two small daughters and he wouldn't just "ask" for something like that again. Dr. Myrtle Baker, a close friend who was a fellow missionary in Tokyo, used to say, "Don't pray to be covered with the blood of Jesus—pray to be kept covered; otherwise it sounds like there are times when we aren't covered."

I agree with her. We need protection and covering constantly, and we should never speak words of death and destruction over our lives, for our words can open doors to evil spirits to act in our lives if we speak in agreement with evil.

Miss Skow lived in the same apartment building as us working girls, a seven-to eight-minute walk from the office. She was a retired nurse, having worked in that capacity her whole life. She did most of her own work; she would visit us often and loved to be in on special things that we did. But there was a strange sad thing about Miss Skow: she was nearly blind.

I said that she did most of her own work: Yes, perhaps because she had lived there so long that she knew just where things were, and she could see a little. However, I remember once that she wrote a letter....and she wrote twice on the same page, having failed to turn the sheet. One day Miss Skow fell down the stairs and ended up in the hospital, but a wonderful thing happened. Doctors operated on her eyes and removed cataracts and she could see! She saw us for the first time before that she recognized us by our voices. Later she wrote me a lovely letter with nicely-spaced lines.

Living with Breta and Ginney as roommates was fun. Ginney liked to have our bedrom window open even when snow was piled high on the outside frame. I decided, "fine, I'm going to be a missionary, so it's about time I learn to accept some things." But the funny part was that Ginney ended up in Africa. Hot Africa.

There were lots of fun times. Right outside our apartment and off the hallway was a stairway to the basement, and it turned at the bottom so you couldn't see all the way down. One day we heard crashing and banging, and Ginney and I rushed out our door and stood at the open door to the stairway, trying to figure out what had happened. From the bottom came Loren's voice, "It's OK. It's just me. I lost my seat!" It struck us as funny and we rushed back into our apartment and headed for our beds and laughed so hard that we couldn't tell Breta about it for a while. Later we realized we hadn't even told Loren we were sorry or concerned. What happened, he explained, was that he was carrying down chairs and the seat of one came off. It made perfect sense.

In the afternoons, we had coffee/tea breaks. Since there were a lot of Scandinavians in this office, they pretty much gave up on me as I didn't like coffee. Never drank it. When one was leaving for other work or another place, that person would treat the office staff to cake or some dessert. One of the girls who was a health food fanatic (which I didn't understand then, but do now) was leaving, so she was to bring the snack. We gals would sit at a horseshoe-type table, and another girl and I were wondering if she would bring some kind of health food. Sure enough, she did bring a healthy dessert and we got the giggles. But we managed to live through it.

During this time I took a short trip to Iowa and met relatives on Dad's side that I never knew. I was ushered in to see an aunt who was having a nervous breakdown. We talked and prayed and I believe she started getting better, because soon I heard she was well.

Back at the office, I was getting ready to set out for Japan. I had been at TEAM headquarters for a year and a half, so I wrote on my quarterly form that I should soon be on my way. Shortly after that, the boss called me in and said that since I was still young, I could stay on at the office for a while yet, but then he chuckled and said that he read what I wrote, and it was fine that I move on. I went back home and then the formidable task of deputation to raise support was before me. Clarence said I was pale when I went to my first deputation meeting. Here and there I spoke, telling people all about a land and people that I knew next to nothing about. It was just after the War, and I guess folks were glad someone was going with the Gospel to that country. We had to raise promises of $125 a month, which were sent into headquarters. Some pledged five dollars, some ten dollars. My Aunt Alice wrote to the family, "Lila stands ready to go, but she needs support."

Deloris Rohe, a nurse from Prairie, was heading to Africa, so we did a little deputation together. She didn't drive, so I was driving across Montana in a desolate area when I noticed in my mirror that there was a car of men right behind us. We had no cell phones, of course, and there wasn't a soul for miles around. I did some desperate praying without telling Deloris, and was mighty glad when the car passed us and went on ahead. Only then did I tell her what I had seen in my rearview mirror.

Another time we were heading across the mountains of western Montana into Lewistown, during winter time. Myrtle was driving and the roads were solid ice. Fifteen miles of this the Lord brought us through and you can't imagine how glad I was when we reached Lewistown and Ray and Myrtle's home.

Little by little, financial pledges came in, and I was soon ready to go, and the Mission made a boat reservation for me to leave from Seattle. Soon I would be on my way to Japan.

CHAPTER ELEVEN

Bon Voyage

Recently, I came across letters that I had written to my parents from Japan. In one, in Mom's handwriting, it read, "Letter #12." On another, "Letter #13." In looking at the dates, I saw that they coincided with my arrival in Japan.

Looking back, I feel it must have been a difficult time for Mom and Dad to let their only daughter go overseas at that time, especially to a country that was our enemy in a war that had just concluded. The morning I left, Mom prayed, "Lord, you know we are both glad and sad today." They wanted God's will for me, but I was leaving home and going overseas.

Dad bought barrels and a pressure cooker for me, as we had to take so much along. Finally, time was up and Mom and Dad took me to Glendive, Montana, to catch the train. That was about 60 miles away. A lot of my family members came to say goodbye, and I walked down the line saying good-bye to 15 or so of them. The last one was Dad. He was openly crying. I had never seen Dad cry before. I was crying, too, and I got on the train and sat down and was on my way. Sometime later a lady sitting next to me asked me where I was going, and I said, "Japan." She said, "I thought so," meaning that it must be more than a mere trip to Seattle. Upon arrival there, I was met by Alma and her brother Ted, who took me to their home, and I was able to attend Alma's graduation from Seattle Pacific University. Future shipmates, Anna Nelson Hamm and Bessie Degerman, also arrived, and we shopped and packed together until it was time to get on the ship. The trip was exciting, and we heard that the crew wondered what we three had done wrong to be sent to Japan! It was a cargo vessel and didn't have many passengers, so we were treated royally.

In June 1954, upon arrival in the Japanese port of Yokohama, we were welcomed and taken to TEAM Center, where Mr. and Mrs. Laug were in charge. Someone in our group said, "Hey, look, there's a sink." Nobody wants to take responsibility for that statement, but I guess to see running hot and cold water and everything so modern was a pleasant surprise. After all, Tokyo had been severely bombed, so we really didn't know what to expect.

After my first letter home, Mom once wrote me, "Well, it doesn't seem like you are so far away, since we got a letter in five days." Direct telephone calls were rare, and there were certainly no faxes or emails. With today's technology, it's hard to imagine that.

Shortly after arriving, I went out to the countryside and visited my Prairie roommate Esther Zerbe and her husband and children for a few days. They had finished language study and were established in a work. Then we three girls boarded a train and headed for the mountains of Nagano prefecture to a little village called Karuizawa, where TEAM sent new missionaries for language study, so it was all set up for us. Learning Japanese before coming was discouraged back then. We lived in a big, two-story house which we quickly dubbed "The Girls' House" and "1413." Amazingly, it's still there and has been kept up nicely.

1413 was a busy place, and we were thankful for it! Much happened there, but most of all we were thankful for faithful teach-

ers so we could learn Japanese well and get to the work where
God led us!

−Anna Nelson Hamm

Here were spent many special days, and lifelong friendships were established. Besides Anna and Bessie, Lorraine Reece and Pat Junker joined our ranks along with Mabel Lindsay, for a while. Japanese teachers came to our rooms and taught us individually. We studied from a course which was taught to the American GIs, and so right off we learned sentences like "Tabako wa doko desu ka?" (Where can you buy cigarettes?) It got you speaking the language pretty early, but not the polite kind. Later when I had moved to Tokyo and gathered some Japanese ladies together for a meeting, I was shocked that I could hardly understand them...their words were so polite and different from what I had studied.

Mr. and Mrs. Yamamoto were our helpers in this big house, and we were especially grateful for them since we didn't know enough of the language to even shop. She cooked wonderful American meals for us, and we ate together in a good-sized dining room on the first floor off the kitchen. There was a big living room that had a fireplace. We girls took turns planning the meals, gradually learning about food and cooking. Mrs. Yamamoto was a happy person and we liked her so much. Everything was new to us. One day, nearby Mt. Asama erupted. We all ran out on the upstairs patio to see what was going on. Down below were some Japanese people looking up at us trying to tell or ask us something. We all stood there mute not knowing what they were saying or what was going on 'til Pat Junker, always the daring one and anxious to use all her newfound Japanese, said to them, "Wakarimasen keredomo, tabun shirimasen," which means something like "We don't know what you're asking, but we probably don't know the answer anyway, even if we did understand." We never let her live that one down!

One day smoke coming from some unknown place made us realize we had a fire on our hands. Not having a telephone, someone ran to a neighbor and eventually a truckful of firemen came. We had just cleaned the house, but they came in with their dirty boots looking for the fire. "Doko, doko (where, where)," they loudly asked. Bessie decided to search upstairs and there she found a closet that housed the fireplace pipes and found the fire. The firemen were up there immediately and put it out with no further fanfare. Except our dirty floors!

One night when Pat Finrow (Clark) stayed with us, we were all upstairs, but were sure we heard noises downstairs. What should we do? Finally it was decided that we needed to go and find out. So, armed with brooms, sticks, and whatever other items we could find, we slowly moved down the side of the stairway, ready to pounce on whoever had intruded, but nobody was there! In all fairness, we did see tracks outside the window the next day.

Lorraine and I have often laughed at an incident that happened one day when we were heading off on our bikes past the Karuizawa train station. Out of nowhere came a good-looking American serviceman and he was clearly happy to see two American girls in this remote Japanese village. We finished our errand and were heading back, when we saw him coming toward us. He greeted us warmly, to which Lorraine answered with some dour firmness, "We're missionaries!" The message was clear: We are not available–stay away!

Karuizawa had not been hit by the war, so it was a delightful place, with luscious greenery all around when we arrived at the end of June. The train ride from Tokyo took about four hours and we went through 103 tunnels to get there. During our time there, we rode bicycles everywhere. Also, at that time none of us wore slacks, but thankfully the hemlines were way down, so our warm coats were good for even our legs. We usually studied with a teacher and by ourselves for about eight hours a day. The evenings found us very tired but not too tired to have lots of fun and excitement and play games.

Since this was the time of year missionaries came to the mountains from their work all over Japan, it was a busy city. Many people had small cottages, or ones that belonged to their missions. Karuizawa Union Church was the gathering place for Sunday morning services, and there were two conferences: An inter-denominational missionary conference which usually featured missionaries, and a Deeper Life conference to which outside speakers came. This was a great blessing for all of us, and we didn't miss many meetings. There was a choir during this time, and I loved singing in that for Sunday services. I also played the piano or organ for meetings here and there.

For a while that year an older Japanese pastor and I rode bikes to a home some miles out into the country for Sunday evening meetings. We met around a kotatsu (hole in the floor for a stove, and then a table over that with a quilt on the table), and I was always glad to stick my feet under the blanket when I finished playing the organ and he had the rest of the service. It was a cold trip, but we bundled up and managed just fine. Before I came, this pastor's wife, who was a teacher to the missionaries, had passed away. Some time later, after we left the area, he, too, died in an accident.

A situation arose in our household which left me devastated. I said to the Lord, "I wish I had somebody to talk with about this problem." The Lord said, "Well you do have somebody." I said, "Who is that?" I heard in my spirit "Japan." I said, "Japan?" "Yes," the Lord said, "How about Lila?" So I knew that was what the Lord wanted me to do and I wrote to her. Interestingly, Lila and her friend had heard about me and were praying for someone to help me. My letter was no surprise to her and from then on we connected with each other by computer. We became prayer partners and shared our joys and hard times, becoming very close, even to this day.

–Inga Skachenko

Me on the farm in 1933.

With my mother, Gunhild "Julia" Finsaas outside of our home in Fairview, Montana.

With Mom, Dad, Ray, and Orvin.

(Left to right) My mother, Julia, brothers Ted and Joe and sister Alma.

With my cousins.   *Getting ready for church.*

Our family: Mom, Dad, my brothers and me.

*I stayed with my best friend
Jean Bond Borseth my
junior year of high school.*

With Jean and the Aarhus twins.

With Mom & Dad at my high school graduation in 1946

I'm so thankful for my time at Prairie Bible Institute

My college graduation photo.

My first prayer card.

Wearing a Japanese kimono shortly after arriving in Japan.

The girls in native garb: Anna Nelson Hamm and Bessie Deggerman.

Waiting for the train:
Anna Nelson Hamm,
me, and Pat Junker.

Members of
"The Girl's House."

Kenny traveled to meet
my parents for the
first time.

My favorite Aunt, Alma, came to Japan to be with me on my wedding day, on her way to Taiwan.

With my bridesmaids on my wedding day.

Our wedding with bridesmaids and groomsmen.

*Kenny and I exchanging vows at the Karuizawa Union church
in Japan September 5th, 1955.*

*Cutting our wedding cake after
exchanging vows.*

*Kenny and I traveled across Japan in an evangelism bus
shortly after we were married.*

Newlyweds.

Missionaries.

Posing with Kimbo and Bobby.

Our growing family, around 1964.

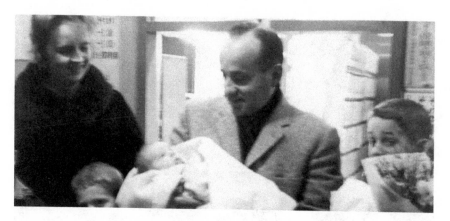

Kenny, the boys and I leaving the hospital with Mark.

Our first photo with our entire family (1968).

Mark and I on my last visit to see my mother before she died.

Leading worship with three of my sons

Our family in Tokyo in 1977.

*Our family in the
United States in 1978.*

*For nearly 40 years,
I played the piano every week
at our home church.*

Bobb's dear wife Georgia joined our family in 1982.

Our last photograph together as a family with daughter-in-laws Cindi & Georgia, and grandchildren Jacqueline, Kerrigan, Reid, & Christopher.

*The Kanji Class
(left to right):
Nancy Suzuki, Joanne
Wright, Kyoko Naito.*

*Reading to my
grandchildren in 2008*

*With my dear
daughter-in-law,
Mark's wife, Kara.*

Celebrating my birthday with dear friends and family.
Back (left to right): Chris McDaris, Beni Polder, Diane Patterson,
Toni Chase, granddaughter Jacqueline, cousin Arlene Riley, niece Pam Watson;
Front (left to right): Pat Clark, Michelle Clark, daughter-in-law Kara

On the set of TBN with host Paul Crouch Jr.

*Holding my 15th and
final grandchild,
Jordan Mark Joseph.*

Relaxing with Kenny.

Enjoying a 4th of July picnic with Kenny after we moved back to the U.S.

One of our last photographs together in 2016.

CHAPTER TWELVE

Unexpected Love

One Sunday morning, as I was singing in the choir at church, I saw a handsome young man wearing dark glasses come in and stand in the back. I immediately recognized him as Kenny Joseph, since we had been in contact with TEAM missionaries back at the head office and prayed for each one by name during our morning sessions. I also remembered that while working in Chicago one day when we were out, one of the girls pointed to a lady and said, "That's Kenny Joseph's Mother." I later remembered that I had written a letter to him on behalf of my boss, as well.

I was intrigued by this dashing young man, but I had decided that I would leave men behind and concentrate on being a missionary. Having just said a firm goodbye to a young man before leaving the States, I was not fair game now. Or so I thought. Still, I couldn't get him out of my mind. So one day I told the Lord that if he was—could possibly be—the one He had in mind for me, to have him come to an evangelistic meeting that night where I was playing the organ. What a shock to me when he walked in the back. He didn't stay long, but he had walked in!

I never told a soul, and actually, when he did start to pay attention to me, he thought I was very hard to get. There were a lot of us singles around at this time, and some busybodies were trying to be matchmakers. One day some of us ended up in a car en route to a meeting, and I was having my first prayer letter printed at a print shop. I got out of the car to work on this, and suddenly Kenny was beside me offering to "help" me. I ignored him, waiving him off, and he went back to the car. He had been pushed by the other missionaries to "help" this new missionary but I wasn't interested.

The first time Kenny came by for me, he took me to one of the few nice restaurants in the area, and when we arrived, the waiter handed each of us an aspirin. I never figured out why as we've never had that experience before or since, but I can only guess that they took one look at us and thought we must have needed something!

The girls at the house were watching these developments, and it became more difficult to step out with him. One evening I persuaded another dating couple to wait for me as Kenny was coming over, and it would take the focus off of us, I thought. She said, "I don't know how this is going to help, but we'll wait!" We were then able to all go off together, making our date a little less obvious.

In November, Kenny proposed, I accepted, and he left on a short trip to the States. My friend Lorraine and I liked to needle each other about our choices. "He's bald!" I said to her about her fiancé Buzz Reece. "Well, at least he's not fat!" she retorted. In fact, Kenny had put on a few pounds, making his clothes a little tighter, largely due to the fact that he had contracted tuberculosis, and a German doctor had insisted that he eat high caloric meals. But the most important thing was that he recovered from that horrible disease.

During that year, we girls studied hard, since three of us had upcoming weddings. Actually, it was a two-year language course, but we finished it in one year. Every six lessons we had an exam, and finally after finishing this course, we had an oral exam before a committee. One person on the committee was at Prairie when I was there.

Our wedding was set for September 1955, and Alma came out in August for a visit. She was on her way to Taiwan to teach at Morrison Academy, which she did for three years. She said that when I was a little girl she used to think that I would make a good flower girl for her. Then, the years went by and she thought I'd be her Maid of Honor. When she didn't marry, she wondered if it would be the other way around: that she would be my maid of honor. And that's what happened and it was so special to have her with us. Suddenly one day we realized that if we waited until September 5th to have our wedding, the missionaries who were there for conferences would all be gone, so we talked about pushing it up to August 24th. I came home from conference meetings one day, burst into Alma's room, and asked her what she would think if we pushed the wedding date up. She had no objections.

First, our friends, Pat and Cal Junker, were married; then Lorraine and Buz Reece; and then finally, us. But at this time a missionary lady was very sick with encephalitis and she died just before our weddings, and it turned out that some of our flowers were used for her funeral. Her parents were on their way back to the U.S. when they got word that Nadine had gone "home." She was in her early 30s.

In time, our Girls' House members scattered around Japan. Lorraine and Buz went to Niigata, Pat and Cal to Matsumoto, and we to Tokyo. The doctor had ordered Kenny not to travel in evangelism like he had been doing, but to have a more quiet job, so he taught at the Japan Christian College, and pioneered the Evangelism Department for five years. This was interesting, because we worked with students, and got to know them. Kenny took them on meeting trips—once to Oshima Island by ship.

I'll never forget the day I walked into Kenny's office and they were talking about a college student who had just committed suicide. Japanese thought of that as an honorable way out of problems. Those Christian students, just about hit the ceiling. To call that honorable—I don't care what the country believes it is simply not so. It is a selfish act that always leaves a devastated family in its wake.

CHAPTER THIRTEEN

Tokyo

Our first house in Tokyo was new, very Japanese and very cold. We had a dining room and table and chairs, but the living room was tatami (rice mat flooring) and we used zabutons (flat cushions) to sit on. I always settled near the pot belly stove when we went to the church near our home. I remembered Clarence, who had been in Japan as a chaplain with the military just after the War, saying that it was so cold in Japan that you even froze with long underwear on.

I wasn't always sensitive and aware in my dealings with the Japanese people. I remember washing clothes and filling the clothes lines with all my big and small, colored, bath towels. The neighbors probably had next to nothing, as it was just after the War. Another time a young man came around to take orders for meat, and I remember him asking me what it really tasted like.

About this time Vivian, my former piano teacher said she needed some assistance, so, I drove about an hour to help her and Don with their move to Tokyo. It was a new area and I got lost, but then found my way out to the right road just at dusk. As I was heading up a little hill, I realized it was a train track and in Japan you're supposed to stop before a train track. But I breezed over it and soon behind me was a police car! Two young policemen came to my window and helped me be sure of my location, and then one said, "But we have to give you a ticket because you didn't stop at that train crossing." I said in a surprised tone, "I've never been on this road before and you're going to give me a ticket?" He motioned with his hand as he said for me to go on and I was thankful for their forgiving attitude!

Vivian also, unknowingly, gave me the courage to start driving in Tokyo. We didn't have a car for our first 10 years or so, but then eventually when we moved farther out, we had one. I had studied Japanese and used it daily, whereas Vivian and Don had been in Japan only a short time. But she drove all over. So I figured if she could do it with her limited Japanese, I could, too, and that got me started.

Even before I was old enough to get a driver's license, I had been driving in America. It was easy in those days in America, but not so in Japan. I passed the written test and then went for a drive with the instructor. I thought this was a cinch since I had driven for years. Upon returning to the base, he told me I didn't pass the driving part because I kept my foot on the clutch too much. Then I realized that I didn't know exactly what was expected of me, so I spent an hour driving with an instructor and then I passed and got my license. It also included a motorcycle license, which of course I never used, but that I think my boys were later envious of.

CHAPTER FOURTEEN

Family

I had eight brothers, was next to the youngest, and had never been alone, but I always had girlfriends, even when working in Minnesota and Chicago. But then I got married, and lo and behold–I was all alone, because Kenny was often away, preaching. That was a new thing for me to get used to and a challenge for a social person like me.

I had lots of friends both at home and in Japan, but we were all far removed from each other. And there weren't a lot of books to help us in our particular situations. And we had no emails! And telephone calls were expensive and rare.

A year into our marriage, I was overjoyed to learn that I was pregnant, and after an uneventful pregnancy, Kimbo was born. Although we named him Kenneth Philip, we soon began to call him Kenbo, and later Kimbo. He was one popular boy with the Japan Christian College students where Kenny taught.

When I brought Kimbo home from the hospital, the neighbor lady came over. At that time, we always had our babies sleep on their tummies, so I had a firm mattress and bed covers for him. My neighbor messed up the whole bed as she was talking to me, fluffing it up so it would be soft. I was still tired, and about this time Kenny came home from school. He sized up the situation and while he kept talking to her, he fixed the bed back the way I had it: firm.

One day Kimbo had colic, and Kenny came home around 1:30 in the afternoon and gasped, "I'm so tired. I gotta get a nap." I said, "You've gotta get a nap and I haven't had breakfast or lunch!" He said, "Oh you poor thing, let me take Kimbo." He did and I went out for a walk. But I remember being so proud I wanted everybody to know, "Don't you know, I have a little boy!" When I got home they were both fast asleep!

Two years later, as I neared the time to give birth to my second, I invited a Swedish missionary nurse to have supper with us one night. En route, she got lost and suddenly there was a Japanese man from the head office of the college that she recognized, so he guided her to our home. After the meal and an evening of visiting, she went home, which was about a mile away. Early the next morning, I called her as I was having light labor pains. She said she'd be right over. But she got lost again, and in her wandering around our neighborhood, who should she meet but this same Japanese man who guided her the night before. He thought she had been searching all night looking for the house, and he blurted out, "Mada desu ka?" ("Haven't you found them yet?")

One day when Kimbo was about two, he looked out the window and said, "takebi." We didn't know that was the word for bonfire! Kimbo, along with our other boys, didn't know Japanese was hard. They picked it up as life went along.

When he was about two-and-a-half, we were in Florida and he and his Dad were taking a taxi somewhere. The driver was smoking and Kimbo blurted out, "He's got fire in his mouth!"

Not too long after that when we lived in an area called Eifuku Cho, a couple named the Brandts visited us from California. After the meal, Bill "lit up" and just as I feared, Kimbo quipped, "He sure must love the devil!" It was quiet so everyone heard it, but Jean, whom we learned later had been encouraging her husband to stop smoking, said as if to underscore that feeling, "Out of the mouths of babes and sucklings…"

About this time when Kimbo was three and Bobby was one, we went on our first furlough. It was Thanksgiving, and many of the relatives were gathered together at my parents' house. They loved to hear Kimbo talk Japanese, and had already heard that he "preached" in Japanese too, so this one evening they begged him to do it for them.

Finally, reluctantly, he got a little book, stood on the piano bench with it open, and said some sentences. Then he closed the book and seriously prayed with closed eyes: "Kami sama, kono warui shukai o stoppu shite kudasai!" Only I understood what he said: "God, please stop this bad meeting!"

One day he announced, "I'll talk Japanese when I get back to Japan!" Because everyone thought it as so cute and laughed, he may have felt they were being rude.

After a stop in Fairview, to visit Mom and Dad, we went on to Chicago where I met my in-laws for the first time.

We spent two furloughs in Florida at the D & D Missionary Homes. It was great to have a roomy house on the grounds, and we could attend various services and prayer meetings–and in English, no less! Kenny's Mother, Martha, even came down and stayed a while and she and I hit it off. I taught her to ride an elevator, and had a birthday party for her with 20 guests. She said it was her first birthday party ever.

Bobby was born on February 27th, 1959, and was an easy baby to take care of. I usually studied Japanese with a private teacher at that time. One day when he was about three years old he was out with a Japanese lady who called home and said that he had been hit by a swing in the face. I expected the worst. I told her to grab a cab and bring him home and then I took the same cab and took him to the hospital. He wasn't really hurt badly, but had a loose tooth. The doctor pushed it back and it stayed until the normal time for it to fall out.

Furloughs were different and sometimes eventful. Once when we were at Bob Jones University, friends of Kenny's decided we needed a night out–a change of pace. So they got a babysitter for their youngsters and Kimbo and Bobby, who were three and one, so we four adults could go bowling.

I put the boys to bed before we left. Bobby slept in a portable playpen that we had along, so he was on "home turf" each night. He was a very good sleeper, so when we got home quite late, I was surprised to hear him crying.

I picked him up and realized he was hot. I asked the lady to feel his forehead. She did and quipped, "Yes, he's got a fever. I think you should give him an aspirin."

But in my heart of hearts, I knew he needed more than just an aspirin, so I asked her if she had a thermometer. She did, and Bobby's temp was 104! She immediately called her pediatrician, and though it was near midnight, he said he would come.

I distinctly remember walking across the room when the verse came to me, "He shall not die, but live and declare the glory of God." That really comforted and stabilized me. When the doctor came and examined him, he gave him the right medication and I held him until his temperature was down a couple of degrees and then put him in his crib where he slept soundly the rest of the night. In the morning he woke up and sat there singing.

Around mid-morning, the doctor called to ask how his patient was and when I told him that he woke up singing, he said, "That might be, but I think he'll break out with Roseola. He was just going into convulsions when I got there last night!"

We were pretty shocked, but Bobby was completely fine and never developed Roseola. So God took good care of us and continued to bless him and uses him for His glory even today.

And by the way, that was the last call the doctor made–after that he went to a hotel where he couldn't be reached. No cell phones in those days!

As the boys got older, it was soon time for Kimbo to attend the school for missionary kids, CAJ (Christian Academy in Japan) on a bus, and for Bobby to enter a Japanese kindergarten. He was the only one who went to Japanese kindergarten, mainly because it was so close by.

When Bobby was between two and three, the boys had a goldfish that died. They buried him in the backyard and there was a little mound to commemorate the event.

One day I saw from my kitchen window that Bobby was kneeling in front of the buried goldfish. I half-jokingly called out, "Are you praying to it or for it?" He promptly answered, "To it." Time for a furlough, I thought to my self.

Jimmy had a hard time getting here and had we not had an excellent doctor and been in a wonderfully equipped hospital, he wouldn't be here and I might not either. Everything was normal until delivery time when my doctor, Dr. Nelson, came and said to me, "The baby is coming chin first and he can't be born that way. We'll have to turn him."

He did and from then on it was easy for me. Jimmy arrived and I noticed Dr. Nelson was checking him carefully. I found out later that he was checking to see if his forceps had been a problem and when he saw that was not the cause of the problem, he breathed a sigh of relief and quipped, "Well, he'll be all right." Then I heard the nurse ask, "This, too?" I wondered what was behind that question: "This, too?" I would soon find out.

When I was back in my hospital room, the nurse brought Jimmy in and he had a bandage on his head. Soon Dr. Nelson came in and told me that Jimmy had a dent on his forehead, but that it was purely cosmetic. Though it was not 8 o'clock yet, he said he had consulted his textbooks, counseled with other doctors, and talked to a surgeon at Yokosuka Naval Base. Dr. Nelson said he had never seen this before, but the Yokosuka surgeon had, so if we agreed, he would do the surgery.

Two days later, Jimmy was taken by a missionary lady to Yokosuka and the surgery was performed with only a small incision in his hair as an instrument was inserted to lift up the dent. Dr. Nelson explained it thoroughly to me, and I was confident that the Lord would guide the surgeon. Kenny expressed his worry with "They're doing surgery on his head!"

Life quickly returned to normal but one day Kimbo and Bobby were practicing their violins when the postman came. He said, "I have a telegram for you. Please sign here." I had never signed for a telegram before, so my first thought was "Who is it?" I knew it was a serious telegram. I opened it up and the first word was "DAD." That was a big shock to us as it was the first death in our family. I know how much he sacrificed in letting me go to the mission field. I was his only girl, yet he released me to serve. I still remember seeing him on the train platform as he waved goodbye and we would only see each other one more time before God called him "home." He suffered a massive heart attack at 77 years old. I was so glad he didn't have prolonged pain.

Kimbo and Bobby came in from play one day and we noticed that Bobby's cute little blue outfit had something wrong with it. This one-piece seersucker material shorts with the little suspenders had a neat cut-out about an inch along the hemline in front. We should have known that they were acting out a Bible story and Bobby was Saul sleeping in a cave when David (Kimbo) came so close that he could cut off a piece of his robe and so prove that he was not out to hurt Saul! Sometimes it's in our power to hurt someone, by a word or an act. We become strong when we refuse the temptation and move on kindness, leaving the judging to God.

One evening we were having guests for supper, but just before they came, Kimbo hobbled out from a closet with a needle poking out of his foot! We rushed to the hospital and I said to amiable Dr. Johnson, "Doctor, do you have boys or girls?" He said, "I've got one boy and two girls and he can raise more Cain then both of them together!"

The next furlough saw us traveling in a motor home that some-one needed to sell. We went to Watford City and stayed with my Mom. She was alone and had already registered Kimbo and Bobby in school there. One day one of their teachers said, "Where have these boys gone to school? They're not behind in anything."

During this time, Bobby missed the first days of elementary school having caught a cold. One morning he thought he was ready to go back to school, so he took his temperature and brought the thermometer to me–still in bed–to check. I jumped out of bed in shock as it registered 104 degrees! He had washed it under hot water!

When we were in Florida once, Bobby was in about second grade and his teacher was impressed with his background in life, so in order to get him to talk she asked the class to tell what their fathers' work was. I guess by the time he heard, doctor, teacher, office manager, and others, he didn't know how to similarly categorize his Dad, so he said his Dad did "nothing."

One year, while vacationing in a favorite spot called Takayama, we had a near-tragedy. The three older boys had gone down to the ocean to swim and I cleaned up our cabin and then went to join them.

But before I got there, Jimmy had gone out in water deeper than he could handle. His friends thought that he was only fooling when he called for help. But Dave Springer, on duty as the lifeguard, saw him struggling and sped out and rescued him from drowning. We'll always be thankful for Dave's quick help.

CHAPTER FIFTEEN

Mission

Our family had grown, and as I took care of the children, Kenny was involved in many writing projects. After his tenure as editor of Japan Harvest was up, he started a magazine of his own in 1961, which he initially called Ripe, and later renamed REAP. As Kenny began to develop REAP over the years, it became clear to both him and TEAM, where he had spent 16 years, that it was time to move on. In 1967, he was allowed to leave and start his own mission, REAP, which stood for Reinforcing Evangelists and Aiding Pastors.

Starting a new mission meant that more support staff would be needed, and soon a missionary secretary, arrived. We treasured our time with Dorcas, who was such a help to us in so many ways as we sought to establish the mission.

It was an answer to my long-held dream of going to Japan with the purpose of serving the Lord in whatever capacity He had for me. It was three months for me to pull enough money together, sell some things, and get the rest packed to go on the boat. We docked in Yokohama, and I was met by the Josephs and my friend, Judy. When we got to Tokyo, the church had a

welcoming party with banners and sukiyaki. Kenny said, "bet-
ter eat up tonight or you will get it for breakfast." So was the
beginning of my wonderful adventure!

–Dorcas Hilligoss Shultz

As Dorcas' time with us came to an end, Kenny and I were blessed by the help and support of another wonderful woman, Bonnie Rose. Bonnie also worked hard, serving as Kenny's assistant.

One summer, I went to a summer training camp and while there, a man on staff shared how he went to Japan to help build a summer camp. He had been guided there through a ministry called Short Terms Abroad. I contacted them and let them know I was interested in going to Japan as a secretary. I surrendered my secretarial skills to the Lord and waited to see how He would guide. Within a few months, I heard from Mr. Joseph. After I got my passport and visa, I was on my voyage to Japan. Immediately, I went to the Missionary Language School to learn the Japanese language. After I learned the basics, I continued with private lessons from one of the Japanese teachers. I recorded my lessons and played them over and over. Before Dorcas left, she asked me if I would take over teaching her English classes. I told her that I didn't know how to teach English. She told me that Japanese people have already learned English grammar. They like to learn conversational English. After I typed letters on the electric Smith Corona typewriter for Mr. Joseph, I would practice my Japanese lessons, visit with the Japanese pastor and his wife, and once a week teach my English classes. I also spent time with Kenny and Lila and their four boys on special retreats and meals at their home. I went to a country I didn't know much about, but I knew God had called me to a land where there were, and still are, many opportunities to share the saving knowledge of Jesus, our Lord.

–Bonnie Rose

In addition to my and Kenny's ongoing work with REAP, we began holding church in our home. You might think it's simple to have church in the home, but I discovered it was a big job. To turn our living room into a church every Sunday meant pulling out the pulpit and setting it out in the correct place, moving the sofas, getting out the folding chairs and making sure they were clean, checking the bathroom to make sure it was clean, and preparing lunch. Usually I made curry and rice for those who stayed behind. Often a couple of girls would stay overnight Saturday and call people reminding them of church. Welcoming people with open arms and making them feel at home was very important. This also included listening to people's problems, and trying to help. Sometimes we would have a good turnout, and other times just a few. One day I thought to myself, "Oh God, you can't even save Japan!" And that very day, in walks a Japanese lady doctor whom I led to the Lord many years before. It was as if the Lord reminded me that it was His business, not mine, how He chose to work in Japan.

After church, everything had to be put away. We contacted people during the week as we were burdened for them. That included visiting homes and hospitals. I would also drive around picking up people for church.

And our little church launched three young ladies onto evangelism ships, the Doulos and the Logos. They went for two years at a time, each of them. One of them met her husband there and they now live in England today, while the other two are back in Japan. Many were surprised that a little church like ours sent out three such "missionaries."

One of the good things about my experience at Megumi Church was my joining the Logos II, where I met many Christian foreign friends. Today I attend church as often as possible and walk with God. Because God supports me during my spiritual crises. I feel peace of mind and I remember those days even now. I am thankful to God for his blessings.

—Yukino Sato

Yet another person who's story intersected with ours was Masako Fujimitsu, whose father worked with Kenny in the early days. When Masako was starting college, she came to Tokyo and lived with us for a year, then after college, became a flight attendant. During that time, she also lived with us before getting married and moving to northern Japan. We have stayed in close touch through the years and she always called us Mom and Dad, and would call Kenny on his birthday. Then suddenly she become very sick and they couldn't figure out what was wrong. They finally discovered that her illness was called Peonies disease, a very rare illness that has no cure. But God moved in, and she began to get well. Little by little she improved so much that last summer she and her husband came to visit us here in California.

When I was a student at a Christian College, I attended worship services almost every day. Before I went to Grace church, I felt the Lord wanted me to go to the nearest Japanese church, but I didn't want to go. While I hesitated, things fell apart in my life. Everything seemed ruined. Then I found a tract in my mailbox informing me that an American missionary was preaching the Gospel in Japanese. I decided that I would go to that church just once. But I was caught by Mrs. Joseph's warm smile. Sometime later, I ended up in the hospital. I stayed there for six months, but I really wanted to die. During that time Mrs. Joseph visited me twice. The helper who took care of me in the hospital saw her and was impressed with her and she changed a lot. She brought me shampoo and took care of me so well. Two weeks after Mrs. Joseph's visit, I could walk and leave the hospital and go back home. That was a miracle. Then Mrs. Joseph invited me to come to her church and every week I got better and better.

—Misako Matsuda

CHAPTER SIXTEEN

Adventures

There is never a dull moment when you're serving the Lord, as I learned many times over throughout the years. Whoever said that missionary life was dull was never a missionary! One furlough some years ago, we were in Texas for a meeting at a church where a good friend attended. Following the directions we received, we drove into the courtyard of the church to get our motor home hooked up for electricity. Kenny went inside to get pertinent information and as I waited, a gentleman named Tom came to talk with me.

"Are you planning to stay here tonight?" he asked. When I assured him that we were, he said, "Then I'll bring you a gun."

I nearly had a heart attack. "A gun? Why?" I blurted out.

With a sweep of his arm over the church courtyard he explained, "Look, if somebody should come to cause trouble, nobody would hear you call." (There were no cell phones back then!)

Tom said we should talk it over and decide what we wanted to do. By the time he got back from driving somebody home. He then added, "You can park your motor home in our driveway."

When Kenny came back, it didn't take us long to decide that we didn't want to stay where we were; so we happily accepted Tom's invitation and followed him to his home, and parked in their drive-way. Tom and Gail have been dear friends ever since. Gail is very computer-literate, and regularly encourages us with articles, tips, challenges, and prayer requests via email.

One of my very special friends was Phyllis Rilling. Phyllis and Emil were on leave from Zimbabwe once when Phyllis and I set out for somewhere, deciding that I would drive going, and she would take the wheel coming back. She was driving when suddenly she decided to make a left turn where she shouldn't have. Immediately from behind came the wailing of a police siren and as she moved to the side of the road to stop, she groaned, "I forgot my driver's license at home!"

A young policeman came to her side as she rolled down the window and reiterated what we already knew...that wrong turn! Then he asked, "May I see your driver license?"

When Phyllis told him her dilemma, he quipped, "Uh, oh—you've got two counts against you," and then stepped away to talk on his walkie-talkie.

My tender-hearted friend was visibly shaken, and I'm sure the policeman saw that from the beginning. He soon came back and relaxed with his two elbows on the window ledge and said, "You're really in luck. I can't find a policeman to write up a ticket, so you'll have to listen to me lecture." He actually seemed to be getting a kick out of it all.

To try to help or at least offer an excuse, I ventured, "She's from Africa, and I'm from Japan." He had a quick reply for me: "I don't care if you're from Timbuktu. She broke the law!"

He then good-naturedly urged us to drive on, without giving us a ticket. I'm sure both of us "foreigners" in America made double-sure we had our driver licenses when we went out after that.

It was 1967, and I was pregnant with Markie as we traveled across America and I began to experience some problems with the pregnancy. In Chicago, I was hospitalized and the doctor thought I would lose him because he said, "I don't know why you women get so upset about having a miscarriage." But the Lord kept him safe and the only change was that I couldn't travel by car anymore. So Mom joined me and we flew to Oregon to visit relatives while Kenny and the boys continued on by car.

Later that fall, back in Japan, we found a new house, and one day I saw Kimbo watching a neighbor lady pour salt over a nearby ledge–an act associated with a superstition in order to avoid accidents. But not anxious to cause trouble with our new neighbors, I asked him, "Kimbo, did you say anything to her?" You can guess what he asked her by his answer, "She said she didn't even believe it, either!"

Bobby was a neat child, but he had a little brother, Markie, who rummaged around in his room while he was at school. Short of locking his door, he decided on another solution. The main problem was a low shelf that held his boxing gloves and other important items, so above the shelf he placed a sign that read, "Please do not touch." The only problem was that the only one who touched it couldn't read!

Another time, Bobby, noticing how much work I had to put in to running a household with four boys, said thoughtfully to me, "If there were three of you, one could rest!"

When Bobby was in 4th grade, his teacher sent home a note saying she thought he needed his eyes checked. We took him to an eye clinic and he was soon wearing glasses–dark-rimmed and elegant ones. What surprised all of us was that a new world opened up to him. Then came the time to switch to contacts. We all suffered with him as he tried hard contacts a few hours a day. What a change when he got soft lens contacts instead. A train ride with young Bobby inspired me to write a poem about our excursion:

Once my Bobb and I were riding on a bus in Tokyo's loop,
It was crowded to the doors and if we tried we couldn't stoop;
All he saw were belts and buckles, but I saw above the throng,

And though the trip was irksome, still I knew it wasn't long.
But my little Bobb was frightened—to be wedged in oh, so tight,
The rest were so much taller, he was just a little mite.
All around him it was darkness and he couldn't see ahead,
He could just stand still and trust me; clinging, waiting to be led.
But he learned a little secret—he'd look up into my face,
And my smile of reassurance would his worried look erase.
Bit by bit the bus then emptied, Bobby saw a shaft of light;
Joyfully he inched out to it, now he knew that all was right!
As for me, I saw a lesson: God is in supreme command,
And though I cannot see or fathom, I will trust and hold His hand;
Though the steps to take are shadowed, and I searched in vain for light,
I'll keep looking in His face—and be assured 'til faith is tight.

Markie was a precocious young boy, but easy to handle. He didn't fuss much and generally took direction well. Once when he was around three years old, he and I were on our way out somewhere, but I couldn't find the car keys. We looked, but couldn't find them. And then we prayed, but still couldn't find them, so I suggested that we go on my bicycle. Markie marched kind of triumphantly beside me as we headed out the door quipping, "God didn't answer your prayer!" Suddenly I remembered that I had left them on the front seat of the car and I jubilantly answered, "Oh yes, He did!"

His teacher said she had teenage problems in first grade when a girl came in crying, and when the teacher asked her why, she replied that Markie told her she couldn't talk to other boys!

Soon we went back to Tokyo and moved into a house in an area called Oizumigakuen, which was our third home. When we were looking for a home to buy near Christian Academy in Japan (CAJ), I made a list of things we would need, and then forgot about it. Years later I found that list, and realized that every item had been met: Big enough for our family, near a railroad station, and near CAJ. All our children attended CAJ by train. We lived there for over 40 years.

Jimmy was five when we moved in, and the lot next to us was

a forest which he dearly loved to meander around. He'd catch little wild animals for his planetarium, and take plants to the neighbor and ask him their names. In that little forest, he loved to putter around with his cap on backwards and he said he wanted to be a farmer. But when Mrs. Kobayashi, our next-door neighbor, spotted Jimmy's latest trophy—a snake he bought at the store—and asked him if his Mother knew he had it...well, his Mother soon found out and he didn't have it very long after that!

But before long the day came when Jimmy stood looking out the dining room windows as workers began tearing down his favorite haunt, the forest. I can still hear his deep inner groan when they slashed the first tree down that Sunday morning. That was the beginning of the end of his forest—replaced by houses.

When Markie was about five, we returned to Japan, after a year in the USA, and one day he and I were on our way to the dentist, whose clinic was a long walk from the train station. As he trudged along holding my hand, he asked, "How far is it, Mom?" Without realizing that he was busy juggling two languages and cultures, I absent-mindedly answered, "Oh, about a quarter of a mile." In a little while he ventured, "How far is it now—about a dime of a mile?"

A few years later, when we were living in California, on furlough, Markie was at a stage where he didn't want to be different from the other kids, so, he told no one that he was born and raised in Japan. His teacher happened to have had a couple of homestay students from Japan the summer before so she was most interested in that country. One fellow teacher was himself second-generation Japanese, so she went to him and began asking him about Japan and he replied, "You have a student in your class who is from Japan. Why don't you ask him?" She did—so the secret was out—and she became a special friend to our family.

It was about this time that Kimbo and Bobby were in college, Jim was in high school, and Markie was in elementary school. The gap in conversation one night showed up when Markie sounded off:

"This is boring!"

Through the years, I enjoyed being a homeroom mother for one of my boys each year. That helped me keep in touch with the students as well as the boys.

"Have lots of friends" was a constant theme at our house! What it really meant was "Don't get tied down to only one girl so you miss having lots of friends during these formative school years." I remember reminding two of them that "you still have at least eight years of school left."

After telling one of them that, the next day I was walking down the hall near the CAJ office and around the corner came one of my boys and a girlfriend. But as if a gun had gone off between them, they hurriedly went their separate ways!

When we were in California on furlough, Jimmy and I were shopping and he took me to the jewelry section and asked me if I'd buy two necklaces for him. One said, "You're the only one," and the other said, "I love you." I told him I'd buy him one, but not both. He dropped the subject and so did I as we moved on.

A short while later I was cleaning his room when I happened upon two small packets ready for mailing. With them was a note to his older brother: "Please mail these two for me, but don't tell Mom." So, I guess they were mailed and the brother never told Mom!

One evening Mark and I had a disagreement—about what, I don't recall. The next morning after he had left for school, I found this note; "Mom, I always tell my friends that if there is a difference of opinion, my mom is always right, but this time you were wrong: you were questioning my motives." I never mentioned that again either!

I tried to let my boys have as much freedom as they could handle and I feel they handled it well. This included riding motorcycles and doing modeling jobs (one of the boys said that he would tell the Japanese group right at the onset of a trip that he didn't drink or smoke, so that was good and settled). Another son said to me once, "Well, you didn't always have the right answers, but we saw your life."

I learned a lot from them, too! One day I was steaming about something and walked into Bobby's room. He could have said, "Mom, cool down!" Instead he came with, "Do you remember those Praise books we used to read?" That was a gentle rebuke I needed to hear. I think we all grew and learned a lot together. I couldn't have loved them more than I did and still do.

At one time, our Tokyo house was badly in need of re-carpeting. So we visited our friend's factory in California, and ordered from what he had in stock. Being a professional, he had no trouble getting it shipped to Tokyo at a reasonable price. We rented a truck and picked it up from Yokohama port and custom's officials were gracious and helpful. But then came the big problem: who is going to install it for us? We contacted a company but their price was $600 per man per day and two men for three days would do it, we were told. But this was way beyond our budget and more than we paid for the carpeting and shipping combined! Then I remembered something interesting that had happened just a few days before.

My friend, JoAnn, and I were sitting in a neighborhood coffee shop when a "foreign" lady (like us!) came in. I had already seen her twice that day. Upon leaving, Jill came over to our table and introduced herself and said that she and her two boys had just moved into the neighborhood from northern Japan.

Shortly after that I searched out her house for a visit and found that she needed stoves, blankets, curtains, and other necessities since belongings she had shipped from her former home hadn't arrived yet. It was November and the nights were cold, so I helped her get the needed items. In our visits Jill mentioned that she had remodeled 10 houses in Seattle while putting her Japanese husband through college.

Later, I thought to myself that if Jill had remodeled 10 houses, she had surely laid carpeting. So I tore over to her house and asked her. "Yes, I have," she assured me. "Laying carpeting is one of the easiest things to do." I told her our problem and she responded, "If I can be paid for the job what one man would get for a day, I will lay your carpeting."

We were overjoyed and Jill was glad to have the income and to make friends in the neighborhood. She worked with professional skill and I worked right alongside her and learned a lot. It was a huge job to lug the heavy rolls of carpet and padding from the garage, but it was sunny, so we laid them out in the road in front of our house, which was on a cul-de-sac. Inside, Jill measured and outside she measured and cut. She knew just how to lift a piece, dig her elbow into it and pull. We pulled and rolled and then we'd drag the right pieces into the right rooms. She ironed splices and carefully laid the rugs so the piling was going in the right direction. Before long the job was finished, and we cleaned up both inside and outside—much to our neighbor's relief.

Jill and her sons spent Christmas with us, but in March they moved back to Seattle. She was in Japan for only four months, but her three-day job lasted us for years. We were so thankful that we could help her, and that she helped us.

CHAPTER SEVENTEEN

Goodbyes

When I said goodbye to my parents in 1954, I didn't know what my future held. I planned to be in Japan long term but who can predict the future? Over the next 15 years I was able to see my Mother only a few times, but we kept in touch through letters. But several years after Dad's sudden passing, she developed cancer, and Mark and I flew back to be with her. Then one morning while I had been home with her for three weeks, the doctor said, "We don't know how long she could live." I had three sons and a husband back home so as much as I wanted to be with her, I knew I'd have to go home at some point. So I returned to Japan and just a week later the telephone rang. How well I remember the day our phone rang at 4 AM. I knew instinctively what I'd hear, and sure enough, my eldest brother said, "Mom just passed away." She had been very sick, so this came as no shock. So it was no big deal, right?

Wrong!

After I hung up, Kenny and I prayed and I fell asleep. But when I awakened at 7 o'clock, I was shocked by my feelings. I felt as though someone had grabbed hold of my heart and twisted it into a knot. Never had I experienced anything like it. But then, never had I lost my Mother, either. Never again would I see the light of day knowing that I had my Mom back in North Dakota. Never again would I go to sleep with the assurance of her prayers. As the day wore on, I realized that Mom was in Heaven with Jesus. Why had I felt so crushed when I first woke up? In my rational thinking I was actually glad that she had gone to heaven, as it could have been a long and drawn-out illness. Then I understood this spiritual lesson: If I didn't have the hope of Heaven, I would indeed be hurting much more than I was. But I knew where she was and where she wanted so much to go, and I was actually happy. Although I wouldn't see her again down here, there is the great hope and assurance of a reunion in Heaven because of what Jesus did for us on the cross.

But I was glad for one thing: I lived my life toward her without many regrets as I'd had lots of chances to help, love, and encourage both her and Dad, even though my time at home with them was comparatively brief after high school.

Though I look back and think of how I could have been more thoughtful, I did write them regularly once a week, and helped celebrate special events by proxy and gifts. On the occasion of their Golden wedding anniversary in 1963, I wrote this in honor of them and my brother, Ray, read it at their celebration.

"Go, young man, go West," they cried,
And the challenge touched his heart,
Those open spaces beckoned so, that he made plans to depart.
But when the family heard it they were filled with great dismay,
They tried in vain to change his mind, and keep him home to stay.
For from the wild and wooly West weird tales had drifted back,
Of evil, violence, and grief there surely was no lack.
"Why, your life's not worth a nickel, Killers roam at will, they say,
"Freely toting guns and arrows, Someone's shot 'most every day.
"You will soon become a caveman if you even find the cave,
"Here the corn is tall and handsome,
There for meager food you'll slave."

But he wouldn't be dissuaded, though he loved his family dear,
Dauntless, brave, and pioneering...he set out without a fear.
To be sure, the West was rugged, Summers hot and winters long,
Some gave up and called it evil, Others found themselves more strong.
Nature greatly joined the testing, Rain was light and drought prevailed,
Grasshoppers in droves descended, Courage ebbed, but never failed.
In the West he lived and loved it, Open skies and wide terrain,
Friendly neighbors—not so vicious—brightened life out on the plain.
There he met his wife of valor, There his children, nine, were reared,
Grew and learned to be resourceful, For they, too, must pioneer.
And they learned a lesson early: goals before us to be met,
Are ne'er fulfilled by dreamy idlers, And quitters never got there yet!
Now this girl he found was pretty and she really caught his eye,
The very first time that he saw her, He went home a-flyin' high.
"You should see that Aarhus girl, boys; A nicer lookin' there can't be,"
And with that old determination, he vowed, "That's the one for me!"
And she it was to share the rigorous, strong in spirit, soul and mind,
For prairie life of self-denial, Few today are to be found.
Many times I marvel deeply that she kept her nine so well,
In an illness she was doctor—checking tongue and pulse to tell.
Keeping all so healthy, frisky; Vitamins were sure unknown,
Canning in the fall the produce, That in spring was always sown.
Dishes washed would total truckloads;
Home-made bread three times a week,
Cakes and cookies, without mixes, for their baker well did speak.
Sure her nerves were worn and tattered,
What one forgot, eight more thought up;
They drove the car into the water,
Blew up the stove with a covered cup.
Two fell in the cellar, scuffling; hit the churn and spilled the cream,
One broke an arm when horseback riding,
Another when swinging from a beam.
But a Higher Power was sought for; Sought to keep and sought to save,
From the world's alluring pitfalls, many hours of prayer she gave.
From the Bible she claimed verses that the Lord would save them all,
Draw them to Himself eternal, Help each one to hear His call.
Hear His call to full surrender; Nothing less than all for Him,

When the heavenly role call's taken, all must be there, saved from sin.
Now the kids are all grown up and scattered far across the earth,
How they all would like to be there on this day to share your mirth.
And to say to Mom and Daddy on your Golden Wedding Day,
"Thanks for all your love and patience as you led us in the Way.
Thanks for discipline and firmness, Thanks for lessons old and new,
Thanks for the tender care and sweetness,
Thanks to God who gave us you!"

Many times I wonder how Mother managed to keep nine children from serious illness, injury, and even death. It must have taken constant watchfulness, been a tremendous strain, required a lot of praying, and probably seemed like a thankless job.

I wonder how she kept everybody clothed in a day when she had to make most everything they wore and without sewing machines. She also had to do all her washing on a washboard. And so many overalls she had to patch up. I know how dirty boys can get, how they go through the knees, and catch their shirts and pants on nails and boards.

I wonder how Mom kept us all fed. She couldn't go to the corner supermarket and load up her basket as we do nowadays. Even I can order Japanese noodles and slurp them up when I'm in a hurry. Without refrigeration, food had to be thought of months in advance. Vegetables and fruit were canned by the hundreds of quarts while they were in season. And Mom never read Adele Davis's "Let's Eat Right To Keep Fit," but still we were fed and fit.

I wonder how Mom could diagnose and treat illnesses like a doctor. She couldn't pick up her telephone and tell her pediatrician about a sore throat, fever, or rash.

I wonder how many dishes Mom washed in her lifetime; how many loaves of bread she baked; how many cakes, pies, cookies, and donuts she made. There were no cake mixes, instant frosting mixes or donut makers, either.

As I've watched my four boys grow, I wonder how she lived through the antics of eight boys. I wonder how she withstood one daughter, especially through those fickle teen years.

I wonder how she was able to say good-bye, so bravely to all of us as each left home for trips, colleges, battlefields, and mission fields. I wonder how many times she prayed for each of us; how many tears she shed for us; how many promises she claimed for us.

But there are some things I don't wonder about, I know:

> *"For her worth is far above rubies...Strength and honor are*
> *her clothing; She shall rejoice in time to come. She opens her*
> *mouth with wisdom, And on her tongue is the law of kindness...*
> *And does not eat the bread of idleness. Her children rise up*
> *and call her blessed; Her husband also, and he praises her...*
> *But a woman who fears the Lord, she shall be praised...And let*
> *her own works praise her"*
> **(King James Version, Prov. 31:10, 25-28, 30-31).**

"...And He will fulfill the desire of them that praise Him."

As I often did during trying circumstances, I wrote out my feelings that helped me cope with my dear Mother's death:

> *He promises wisdom...He promises strength,*
> *He gives it out freely when mine is all spent.*
> *He shares all my burdens when none else may care,*
> *He lifts and He comforts; He answers my prayer.*
> *He yearns over sinners so bent on sin's path,*
> *He sends prods to turn them away from God's wrath;*
> *He raises up loved ones and good friends who dare—*
> *To pray and to plead 'til there's answer to prayer.*

CHAPTER EIGHTEEN

Service With A Smile

When Mark was of school age, Kenny and I decided that I should take an opportunity to teach at a prestigious Japanese university, Nichidai, which is short for Japan University—one of the top universities in Japan. One of the professors there knew Kenny, and had asked if he would teach English. Kenny initially turned him down because it was a time of real turmoil in Japan with anti-American campus protests happening, and he was concerned for my safety. I wasn't afraid, though, because I reasoned that they wouldn't touch a woman. So I decided to do it and ended up teaching two years there. But trouble ensued when I refused to give students As if they wouldn't show up for class, something they were not accustomed to. They were used to skipping and still receiving good grades with other professors, but not with me. My students were mostly young men with a smattering of young ladies who usually sat in the front row.

Once we had a bit of a scare when one of my students began attending our church, and suddenly proved himself to be mentally unbalanced. He began to threaten our family, and once sent us a postcard in which he had drawn a picture of our house after he had set it on fire. In large English letters he had written across the burning image of our home, "FIRE!"

Stories like that were the exception, of course, for we had many good experiences with many Japanese, who saw their need for Christ. And because we were in Japan for the long haul, they knew they could trust us. It's not like we had come yesterday, and didn't understand. They knew that we understood, and so they felt like they could come with their problems.

> *If I have a problem, Mrs. Joseph gives her heart to me and my burdens are lifted. She shared the Gospel with me, and I have grown in my faith.*
>
> **–Chitose Ozawa**

These people would open up, and often we were able to help them see what the problem was. Their hearts were really hurting, sometimes, because of unfaithful husbands. There was a common thread running through the lives of people, and once you touched that thread, you could get to their inner source and find out what's causing the problem.

One day I picked up the phone and the girl's voice on the other end said, "Hello, this is Reiko." Her English was perfect. I had only met her once or twice before.

I blurted out, "Reiko, have you been in America?"

"Yes" She said "I studied in a Christian school for a year."

The months passed and eventually Reiko came and stayed with us. She was working downtown. One morning she and I were having breakfast when she shocked me with, "Well, today I think I'll commit suicide." She said this as if she were going on a picnic. I was stunned so I put aside everything for the day and spent time with her.

She said, "When I came back to Japan, it was as if a cloud came over me. I never had that feeling once in America. And I just wasn't able to handle that."

The Lord met her and she is serving Him today.

One day I dropped in at a lady's house where my boys were teaching her sons English. These were wealthy people, really nice people, and this beautiful, classy lady said to me, "Do you believe in demons?" Before I could answer she went on to say, "The demons come to me every night, and they are trying to kill me." I had never heard of anything like that before and our experience with that family opened our eyes. Here was someone whom we got to know personally, someone who was obviously, and by her own admission, demon-possessed.

One day, she said she had been given three spirits, and she gave me the names of them. I wrote them down. She started to come to church, and she would have seizures during the service. On one occasion, she and her son were in church, and this beautiful, well-dressed lady went into a trance. Kimbo, maybe wasn't feeling well, was upstairs in his room, and church was going on downstairs, so I rushed up to him and said, "Kimbo, are you strong enough to help me?" I didn't mean physically–I meant spiritually. And downstairs, she was in the middle of a spasm, where the demons would just take control of her and talk through her. I had never experienced anything like that. So Kimbo came, and we were talking and telling the demons to leave her and then Kimbo asked, "Why won't you leave her?" And through her voice we heard, "Because we still have work to do." Kimbo asked, "What kind of work?" and they said, "It's too bad. We won't tell you."

We knew an older experienced Christian, Canadian lady who was a chiropractor, who lived not so far from us, so I thought of calling her, but she didn't speak Japanese, so I said to Kimbo, "Ask them if they understand English." He asked and the reply was, "If it's about God, we don't understand it even if it's in Japanese!" Finally, Kenny came and we prayed with her. She had accepted the Lord at one point, and she'd bring her Bible to church and had it really marked up, but then one day she told me, "I am a Christian, but our home is Buddhist, and so we're going to have to follow that." She stopped coming to church.

One day she came to a ladies' meeting at our house, and there was another lady there who was mentally ill, and looked like she had picked her clothes out of the waste basket, whereas this lady was impeccably dressed, with expensive clothes. The one who was poorly dressed was pregnant. Strangely, shortly afterwards, the well-dressed one called me after she got home and said, "I'm in a terrible condition." I said, "Ok, I'll be right over." And so I jumped in the car, and I went over to her house. She was simulating pregnancy, saying her back was hurting like as though she was expecting. Somehow or other, the demons from the pregnant lady had come on to her! This was all new to us, as we had never heard of anything like this before. I thought, "I can't deal with this," so I decided to take the two women to see my experienced missionary chiropractor friend and have her pray for them.

We got in my car, and suddenly I had two flat tires right in front of her garage. I had only had one flat tire in my entire life, and that was back in Montana. It was as if the enemy was trying to stop us. We began walking back to the well-dressed woman's car, so she could drive us. All this time we were walking, she was rubbing her back like she was eight months pregnant. We got in her car and went to the chiropractor's house. She joined us in prayer and then a man came over from the church and prayed for her, too. And at one point, she said, "They left!" and she swept her hands in the air.

She got one of these spasms when she was in the car. She clenched her firsts as if to hit me, but she somehow kept tight control. She knew the names of the "gods" she had been given, and they spoke through her.

So we knew for a while there that we had stepped into dangerous territory where we weren't wanted. Eventually she had a measure of deliverance, but she didn't want to pay the price of serving God fully. They were wealthy people, and they had everything going for them, but they ended up with a divorce. Her husband died and they lost their home. But that really opened our eyes to understand things in the spiritual realm that we had never understood before.

Once I met two sisters who told me that when they get together, the demons would talk to each other and it would make them want to vomit. So finally they put a stop to that, and when they put a stop to it, it would make her sister run to the bathroom and vomit to get rid of them. She kept telling them to leave her. She would say it like she was gagging. All of this made us aware that there is spiritual warfare, whether we see it or not.

> God's Word was shared everyday in the Joseph's home. Many people have deep hurts and needs that they can't share with their friends or families; these things are usually never talked about. We are so blessed materially and we have everything that we need, but in our hearts, there is something missing. People lack compassion and love, but something happened in this house that changed people's hearts. People come to share their feelings with Mrs. Joseph, and she really understands, and she shares like nobody else can. By talking with her, people can find, through the Word of God, what's missing in their hearts.
>
> **–Harumi Kato**

Another time, I got a call from a woman who had just come from America and was living downtown. The reason she called was because of domestic violence, and she didn't know what to do. I asked her if she could get on a train and come to our place. She said she couldn't because she had a black eye and a broken toe! I asked, "Do you have some sunglasses?" to which she replied that she did. And the toe, well, she could walk on it. I picked her up, and we took her out for dinner. She was a delightful lady, and we had a great time getting acquainted with her.

When we got home, I showed her to the downstairs bedroom, and eventually we all turned in for the night. She asked if she could call her husband to assure him that she was ok. For some reason, I got up in the night and went downstairs, something I rarely do and saw that her light was on. It was midnight. I went in and she was lying in bed with the phone in her hand. I asked her who she was talking to and she said it was her husband. Obviously, this call had gone on for hours. I slipped the phone out of her hand and told him she was in bed and going to sleep, so good night! She said his talking switched from nice to cajoling, to mean, but he wouldn't let her go. Since she was an important writer for a major American newspaper, this was even more difficult to understand. It turned out that she had married this man too quickly. He was married and had two children when they met on a trip to New York. He came back to Japan and divorced his wife, but, understandably, he missed his kids.

She stayed with us for a few days until her brother and sister arrived from New York. I was impressed with their family unity – when one was hurting, they dropped everything to come and help. One day I went with her to her apartment under police protection. During that time she was with us she kept getting calls from some-one in Bangkok, so I asked her who that was. "Oh, that's my broth-er," she said. "He and his wife are missionaries over there." Well, we have lots of cult missionaries and I wasn't sure what group they might be with, so I asked her. When she told me that they were with King's Garden Ministries, I was jubilant and whooped, "Oh, they've been praying for one more in the family to be saved, and it looks like it's going to be you!" I knew that was a good organization because my aunt and uncle taught and worked there.

When her family arrived in Japan, they took over and went back to the U.S.. She and her husband were soon divorced, and she even-tually remarried. We often saw her articles in the paper, and though we've lost contact, we trust she has come to know the Savior of her brother and his wife.

Lila-Sensei seems like "kuuki" [air]...Because like air, she is
always here. I can always depend on her to listen and talk with
me if I have a problem. There's always an assurance in my
heart that she's here, and I can call or come by. She's like my
own mother, my number one best friend or a very close rela-
tive.

–Kimiko Sawada

I've had many "daughters" on the mission field and I was especially fond of one of them, Junko. When she would come to visit and
play the piano so beautifully, I would sometimes be moved to tears,
thinking of the difficult road she had traveled and the part that God
had allowed us to play in her life.

Once I had just gotten back from America, and was looking at
the clock to see how soon I could justify going to bed so early because of my jet lag. Suddenly the phone rang, and it was Junko saying that she had been locked out of her home. She lived two hours
away, so I told my husband that I would have to get on trains and go
to help her. When I got there, we went into the home together, and I
was quizzed by her husband as to why I was there, but the incident
blew over. Junko had many of episodes like that. This lady who used
to work in the Prime Minister's office, was a piano teacher, a beautiful and dedicated Christian, and a skillful maker of hand ornaments.
But she had a marriage that was in shambles, and she felt helpless
to change anything. When it seemed as though her very life was
at stake, when some of the terrible headlines we read about today
might be a possibility, Junko moved into our spare downstairs room,
and for over a year commuted to a job two hours away.

After a year, when the marriage was officially over, Junko moved
back to her home country and began life with her parents. The years
have flown by, and her three children are grown up now– one is a
registered nurse, one a teacher, and her son is a company worker.
As adults, they are understanding, and love their Mom. They also

take good care of their Dad. It was a trip to see her first grandchild that brought her back to her family. And to us. Recently I enjoyed hearing her talk about the necessity to learn to be joyful and happy and praise the Lord in spite of problems in life. She's learned it well. She is a vibrant person…and I'm thankful she's our "daughter," even though we joked that this new baby–her grandchild–is our great-grandchild! Am I that old?

"What a beautiful girl!" was my first reaction at seeing Yoneko many years ago. She was then about 19 years old, and a student at the Christian college where my husband taught. But soon I realized there was something drastically wrong with her. The girl with the beautiful face had no legs and was missing an arm! Her life had been fairly normal until she was 16, when her mother died. This is a shock to any home, but to a Japanese home perhaps even more so. Fathers often leave early in the morning and get home late at night, so to the mother falls the family, home, community affairs, and handling of money. So Yoneko came home from school to a dark, empty house. There was no warm welcome, no table spread with the evening meal–only emptiness in the house and in her lonesome, aching heart. How she longed for her mother's understanding presence. Eventually her father, older brother, and sister would come home, and together they would get the evening meal ready and the necessary work done. But as the days went by, they sensed Yoneko's extreme depression. They tried to be cheerful but it didn't help. She began to hang out at a roller-skating rink with other restless young people and this soon led her to smoking, drinking, and skipping school. All of this was unknown to her family.

As the ache persisted, one thought began to dominate her mind: suicide. Guided by dark, unseen forces, Yoneko finally made her way to a train station in the heart of Tokyo where she brought her horrible plan to fulfillment: she threw her body onto the tracks just as a train was approaching.

It was no accident that when the train threw open the emergency doors, a man standing nearby held a rope and with a deft, well-timed leap, rescued her and tied the rope above severed limbs to keep some measure of blood in her mutilated body until more help arrived.

Soon Yoneko found herself in a hospital bed but this was no comfort to her as she had gone to such extreme lengths to try to die. It wasn't until she went to take some pills that she found out that three of her fingers on her right hand were gone. Then she realized that her left arm from the elbow was gone, and when they rolled up the bed, she fell forward, realizing that she had lost both legs at the knees. Now her despair knew no bounds, and she began to plan another dark scheme.

Though death had cheated her once, she decided to try again. She began to stash away the little white sleeping pills, putting them here and there so no one would find them.

However, during these dark days, a missionary—together with a young Japanese man—began to visit her. They sang and read from the Bible. Yoneko wasn't even courteous. She didn't even want to be alive, to say nothing of entertaining visitors but each week they came. She liked the singing, but nothing about Christianity. They brought her a cassette tape, and it was while listening to that, that she made her decision to ask Jesus to come into her heart.

On a subsequent visit, the two asked her to pray. She did, and they left. The next morning Yoneko awoke a new person. Gone was the pent-up bitterness, frustration, and hopelessness. Instead, her life was filled with peace and love. She decided it must be a miracle because she had reached out to a living God, and He had touched her. She decided she had to tell somebody, so she told her roommate. Jesus Christ had heard her prayer, come into her life, and made her a new person. Her happy disposition was contagious, and she learned how to do most everything as before, despite her handicap. She went to the United States and was fitted with artificial legs. She later married and had two beautiful daughters who attended school with our sons.

Living as a foreigner in a foreign country makes one aware of interesting and fun traditions and customs. "Your rabbit got out and the next-door neighbor brought him back—better give her a gift," was the greeting my friend gave me when I got home one day. Invited guests, or those who just "appear," always come with a beautiful bouquet of flowers, fresh fruit or something equally special in Japan. You will do well to remember to do the same when you are the guest. Businessmen—though coming to see the man of the house—usually bring a box of cookies, crackers, or a tin of fragrant tea for the family. Not only must a bridal couple think of their own needs, but provide an attractive shopping bag of gifts for each family that attends the wedding, as well. This bag usually contains one nice item, like a lacquered plate appropriately inscribed for the occasion, and a small lunch. A similar surprise awaits each one attending a friend's recital. Some freshly-made cupcakes or a plate of cookies taken to a neighbor are always reciprocated with something special and the plate is never returned empty. Even the bereaved are not exempt as it's customary to take a gift of money to the closest relatives just before a funeral. But then in the weeks that follow, they will return to each giver an item worth about one-third of that amount. Middle-of-the-year gifts are the order of the day for those you're indebted to, like a teacher, and there's another gift at the end of the year.

CHAPTER NINETEEN

Free At Last

At an important time in our missionary lives, we had a crisis. Kenny had purchased a building for the mission, and after several years had agreed to sell it to a Japanese pastor, so that we could move to a new home. Somehow, there was a misunderstanding between the two, and we found ourselves in the middle of a lawsuit with this pastor. This, of course, affected Kenny, who wouldn't listen to some members of the missionary community who believed he was in the wrong. Once when a group of them came to admonish him, he sent them all home licking their wounds, because he knew all of their problems. I realized something had to be done. I am surprised that I had the guts to do it, but I took Markie, who was now eight years old, and we secretly traveled to America. I wanted to talk to the board and tell them what was going on, since they weren't doing anything. Markie and I arrived in California, and we spent a couple of months in the USA.

Once there, our chairman, Hal Morr, and I traveled to Chicago and left Mark behind with some friends. There must have been five or six board members. I didn't know them all but when they heard my story, they all resigned instead of facing the problems head on.

At the end of the summer, Markie and I traveled back to Japan, and Kenny and the other boys were there to meet us. Kenny never said a word about it, but it must have been strange for him. Still, life went back to normal again at least for a time. But after the mass resignation, a new group of men in California took over the board. I remember during this time, as Kenny sank further and further into depression and anger, once Bobby said to me, "You know, we don't have to take this." But we soldiered on.

I came to realize that we were in a supernatural battle between forces that wanted Kenny to thrive, and those that wanted to destroy him. Many of us Christians had been taught in Fundamentalist circles that a Christian can't be bothered by evil spirits. We used to sing when I was a youngster, "The devil's deserted and I've been converted." What a joke, I think today, because we find people with all kinds of problems and they're going to psychiatrists, and they're not getting any help. And the reason is that they haven't learned that we're in enemy territory, and we have to take authority over these problems on a spiritual level.

Through the years I'd seen Kenny go down, down, down, down, and we would just see him helpless to stand against the tide. Kenny often considered the people who tried to help him as enemies, and many people had tried to talk to him with no luck. We returned to the USA, and went together to a Christian counselor as a family. The counselor said to all of us that we had to assert ourselves more, and stand up and show signs that we were learning. But nobody seemed able to help him. Kimbo tried many times, and he was the only one who was a match for his Dad, but they never really got anywhere. But he really tried. And one night they were talking in the living room, and they got pretty loud. Kimbo said, "Mom, can I call Dr. Murphy?" And I said, "I don't know? Who is he?"

He explained to me that he was a professor at Talbot Seminary who dealt with spiritual warfare. He came over–it was 11:30 at night. He talked with us for quite a while and prayed. But then he went home and I think that was when Kenny really realized that a work in his life had began.

A few weeks later, we set up an appointment and he came over again. And he was a tremendously understanding man who said, "Kenny have you ever thought that this is your problem, that it's demonic?" And he explained it and he said, "You don't want to be like this. I believe you are a godly man and you have purpose. But you are constantly pulled." And he brought up rejection and retaliation and rebellion. And he said, "You're constantly thrown from rejection to rebellion, aren't you? So you think everybody is against you. And then so you're going to fight. So, you're thrown back and forth." He explained, "You can take authority of this yourself, over these areas in your life," and with that he left us. Still, we were kind of disappointed because we thought that he would be able to help us more.

But the next morning Kenny read an article about General Wainwright, an American prisoner of war in Japan who had been tormented by the Japanese mercilessly, until one day when they received the news that the war was over. Wainright, reduced to skin and bones, stood up strong and told his captors that he was now in command.

As Kenny read the article, all of a sudden it was like the scales fell off his eyes and he understood that he had been a prisoner of all these evil forces that had been mastering him. And so together we just took that authority back. And the reason this wasn't a flimsy experience was because it was foundational. It's something that you walk in day by day. So, almost every day we would just stand and take authority and name these all over again, and just take authority over them. I remember that vividly because he came to me and said, "This is a tremendous article." Somehow it had just gotten clearer to him and God used that article to change his heart. He had had bad feelings toward many people, but very soon he went back to Japan and apologized to each one. Then he apologized to each member of his family, one by one. God was working in his heart.

The Lord brought us into a wonderful new light when we were right at the end of our rope, really, thinking that there was no reason why our family should live like this. But the Lord, through all this time, had given me some wonderful promises of what he planned to do. You know I was thinking about doing an article called "God is not in a Hurry." We want everything instant these days, but God isn't in a hurry.

We were reading the story of Joseph—one morning, before all this happened, and Kenny had said, "You prayed for so & so—why didn't you pray for me?" So, I said, "Okay, I will pray for you. I will pray for you according to this verse the Lord has given me for you in Psalms, where it says, "Joseph was bound…and kept in prison until God's word came and then he was set free. And he was put in charge of all kinds of work." And I thought he'd blow up at me and he didn't. And then he prayed, "Thank you for your Word, Lord."

Then, over the next couple of days, we went to the beach and read that whole story of Joseph, and what impressed me was that for 30 years Joseph's father didn't know that his son was alive. All those years God let him suffer. Now He could have whispered to him, "You know your son's alive—he's okay." but He didn't. And then the brothers came back from Egypt and said, "Okay, your son's alive. Let's go see him." Then God said to him, "It's okay for you to go." Now, where was God all those 30 years? But that's the way God chose to do it. And I was really impressed by that. God isn't really in a hurry; He just takes his time and works according to His purposes.

I remember one morning waking up and just as clearly as day the word came to me, "I will do a work in your day that you wouldn't believe it though a man told it unto you." When I told a friend about this she said, "That's what's kept you going." Throughout my life, God's promises have been so unusual. There is a verse in Isaiah that I've often come back to: "For I am offering you my deliverance not in the distant future but right now I am ready to save you." And there's another place that says, "My mercy and justice are coming soon. Your salvation is on the way."

And so God just gave us this encouragement all along the line to keep us steady until He really moved in and gave us a new start. The changes in Kenny were both instantaneous and gradual; instantaneous in the sense that God provided a miraculous deliverance, but there were also personality traits that had been developed over the course of a lifetime that had to be slowly changed. I felt like Kenny was in a way starting over, but not alone—with his whole family. I really did praise the Lord for that. Each one of my children had been concerned for their Dad, and they rejoiced to see him come into victory. There were times when I had thought, "It's a hopeless situation." But then we stepped into a great ministry and saw God's miraculous leading and I thought, "You know, God can do more in a second then men can do in years." And people around him began to be affected by his change. Mark's attitude toward his Dad changed. But the Bible says, "A brother stumbled...offended is harder won then a city," and it took time for others to see the change. And it wasn't always that easy, and I had to learn patience over and over again.

When we had come back to the United States that time, I wasn't sure we'd ever go back to Japan, or what our future held. But as Kenny was delivered from the chains that bound him, we began to pray and seek God's will, and it was clearly impressed upon us that we were to go back for a new season of ministry. So in the summer of 1979, we packed up our things, sold our house, and moved back to Japan.

CHAPTER TWENTY

Back In Japan

Kenny and I returned to Japan with Jim, who was a senior in high school, and Mark, who was to start the sixth grade. Kenny found new avenues of ministry, writing and evangelizing, as well as pastoring our church while I continued to work with women, mentoring and discipling them. I also found time to sharpen my Japanese skills and deepen friendships with fellow missionaries through a class that studied Kanji, or Japanese characters. Through that I developed lifelong friendships. Our teacher not only taught us Japanese, but would take us to interesting places for lunch. We studied hard and enjoyed our time together. As I went to class each week, I met and became friends with many wonderful ladies, including our teacher, Kuniko Naito.

One day in April we were in a park reading under full-bloom-ing beautiful cherry blossoms and had petals in our coffee cups. Nancy-san from Hawaii was a genius at finding impor-tant information to enrich our program. One day we celebrat-ed Lila-san's birthday in a plaza in Shinjuku with a beautiful carrot cake JoAnn-san made especially for that day! We visited

the Sapporo Snow Festival too and were brave enough to walk
through a snow storm with our arms linked together so that we
wouldn't be blown away. I felt we were a very special group
with Lila-san like our eldest sister always caring about us.

–Kuniko Naito

Also during the week I taught at many jukus ("cram" schools), and once I rode my bike about two miles to get to the school where that juku was.

After Jim went off to college in the USA, Kenny and Mark and I lived for the next six years together, as a smaller family unit, with occasional visits from our older three sons. Those years were spent in continued ministry, with Kenny traveling to India, South Korea, and many other places spreading the Gospel. Kenny also enjoyed faithfully attending Mark's basketball games, and etched in my memory was the time that he was filming one of Mark's games and someone told him that his son had just broken the school record of most points in a game, when Mark had scored 44 points! Our family had been brought low in the missionary community for a time because of our troubles with the lawsuit, and I know it was a great measure of joy for Kenny to see that same community see his son's exploits on the basketball court.

When Mark went off to college, Kenny and I were empty-nesters once again, and for the next 20 years we enjoyed a wonderful season of ministry, with Kenny performing weddings, writing articles, traveling for evangelism, and staying active in the community. We gathered for the last time as a family in 1994 when we took our final family picture together at a mini-reunion of sorts in Oakland, California, where Bobb lived at the time.

God has promised me a new season of fruitful ministry and life, if I would be faithful to Him and His Word. Trust me, more than one person had suggested I should throw in the towel on our marriage during our darkest hours. But I had no interest in that. I was committed to God and my husband and there was no way I would ever walk away from the vows I made to both of them. As I look around today, I see many Christian women who give up on their husbands and their marriages. I sympathize with them, of course, but I am a living testimony to the fact that if you will honor God's Word and refuse to give up, God will work in miraculous ways. Because I didn't give up on my marriage and remained obedient, God kept His promises to me and to our family. He can do the same for you.

CHAPTER TWENTY-ONE

The Last Time

I've so enjoyed sharing my story with you, but all good things must come to an end, and this book is slowly come to an end. This is the last chapter, and just like a book has a closing chapter, so do our lives in so many ways. Have you ever wondered when you did something for the last time? Like when was the last time you drove that yellow sports car before your friend totaled it? When was the last time you rode a tricycle? Or a bicycle? When did your acne stop? Or when did you give your baby his last bottle? When didn't Janey need diapers any more at night?

Sometimes we know when things terminate. We usually can recall the evening Aunt Sally's visit ended and we said "good-bye" to her at the airport. Everyone seemed to be crying. Or we can pinpoint the day Uncle John had his accident. And sometimes we distinctly say to ourselves, "This is the last time I'll be walking down these halls" or, "This is the last evening I'll be 18 years old."

Then there are times when we may be aware of the fact that we are in the process of a "last." After spending three weeks with my ailing mother, I had to leave. Though she was much improved, her 77 years made for an uncertain future. And my home was 6,000 miles away in Tokyo. As I reached the door of her hospital room after a tender good-bye, I deliberately turned and looked at her lying there in her white hospital clothes. I was quite sure that it was a final look. It was. She passed away a week later.

Another time I remember walking through our upstairs hallway thinking, "This is the last night my four boys will be sleeping in their own rooms for some time." Morning was to be a parting time and when crossing an ocean is involved, it's no small matter. Other times we plan a "last." "Let's get together once more before Jeff leaves," we might say. Or we invite friends over for dinner before they move away.

Usually, though, the "lasts" slip by unnoticed. Nothing warns us. Nobody screams, "Hey, you're doing this for the last time!" or, "You'll never see that again." You come home one day to find that the next-door neighbors have moved out. So trivial. But still you wonder when you saw little Jerry's bike out front the last time. Or heard Ann, the loud, happy teenager yell, "Everybody, I'm home!" like she always did.

At 17, when I went away to school, we used lamps. When I came home for vacation, electricity had moved into the countryside where we lived. I wonder when I lit the lamp for the last time. Or washed the sooty glass chimney. Or saw a bug fly into the mantle on the lamp. On the farm we had to get up early and pick raspberries when they were in season. Mosquitoes were bad sometimes, and we really didn't enjoy the procedure all that much. In time the raspberry bushes all froze out. I wonder when was the last time we kids and Mom geared ourselves up against the biting pests and filled buckets of the red berries.

Last times are often scheduled, but we've forgotten them, too. What adult remembers the last day of fourth grade? Or even the last time you slid your feet under your desk as a graduating high school senior?

Like it or not, we must contend with lasts as part of growing up, of changing, and living life. Far from being a morbid preoccupation, the thought of lasts should be directed toward ourselves and our relationships with others. Life moves on and certainly one day will be our last. We should prepare for it.

Once a shopkeeper told me that his wife recently died after being hit by a car. Little did I realize when I saw her for the first time a few months ago, happily working in the store, that I was also seeing her for the last time.

Certainly keeping in mind the possibility of lasts should make us more thoughtful. More considerate. Will others remember us because we cared and took time to help? Not all the lasts have happened yet. We have chances to affect them by our daily living.

And in the last several years, my life has been full of many "lasts." One of those big "lasts" was saying goobye to my beloved Japan. It all began in 2012 when there was a major earthquake. Kenny was upstairs and I was downstairs doing other things when the shaking began. I felt there was something different about this one, and I've lived through hundreds of them. I went out the kitchen door and looked at our yard, which was rocking back and forth. I'd never seen that before.

Not long after it had passed, I became quite ill and began to have panic attacks, something completely new to me. For some time now my Japanese doctor had suspected that I had the onset of Parkinson's disease, but when I went into a specialist for more tests he said: "If it's Parkinson's, it's very mild, but our machine is broken, and it can't be used until next week."

We went home, but I kept feeling worse, and actually began to wonder if I could last another week! Finally, feeling increasingly desperate, I emailed Mark and Bobb in America, asking them to "please come and get us!" Since this was a first, from someone who could handle most situations, they knew it must be serious. Kenny quickly agreed, and he and I were soon on our way to Southern California to stay with Mark and Kara and family, and be under the care of excellent doctors there. To have me come in a wheelchair and be hardly able to walk was a shock to them, I'm sure.

I had never connected my anxiety attacks with the magnitude 9.0 earthquake that hit Japan that spring, but one of the first questions my American doctor asked me was, "When did you begin feeling this way?" to which I replied "Two and a half months ago." He then asked me when the great earthquake was and I replied again "Two and a half months ago." It was an "aha" moment to be sure. CNN has since reported that as many as 30% of Japanese have been hit like I was emotionally after that great quake.

Being back in the U.S. allowed me to consult with several specialists about my Parkinson's diagnosis. Although it had been nearly two years since it was first suspected, I hadn't received any medication for it in Japan and consequently my walking had been reduced to shuffling. My American doctor quickly put me on some very effective medication which made a dramatic difference and I then visited a second specialist who introduced me to an experimental drug that isn't available in Japan, which actually is thought to have the potential to stop and even reverse the disease. I'm so fortunate to have such excellent care, and see both doctors regularly in the hopes of reversing this condition.

Kenny and I settled into a new life in Southern California. Mark and the chairman of our mission, Mr. Turner, had been able to purchase a wonderful three-bedroom home in a beautiful community with many others in our age-bracket, and we enjoyed five beautiful years there. Kenny enjoyed going to the jacuzzi nearly every day, and we had many fun evenings with members of our community. And, of course, we spent as much time as we could with our beloved grandchildren.

Still, I wasn't feeling well and was determined to receive a healing either through doctors or the Great Physician, or both. Mark took me to several places to be prayed for, joking that we should be prayed for by Charismatics, Evangelicals, and African-American believers to cover all of our bases! One of those was Mark's dear friend, Andraé Crouch. Five years earlier, Andraé had graciously traveled to Japan to sing at my 75th birthday celebration at our home, and he ministered to us in such a powerful way. This time it was my turn to visit his church and asking me up on the stage after his service, he asked how I was and I shared openly with him the great physical and emotional challenges I was facing. He took my hands and prayed the most beautiful prayer over me:

> *We come to you as humble as we know how. And God we thank you that you have servants that before the hoopla of being a missionary was popular or anything you called them to Tokyo. She and her husband as young people. God, you called them there and they said yes. God, you have not forgotten them and God I pray in the name of Jesus right now that the Holy Ghost, as we used to say—as some people used to say years ago—they wouldn't even mention that today. God, we thank you for the name Jesus, for the fruit of God, the Holy Ghost, we pray right now that you should surge through this body in the name of Jesus. You said that you would. "Lo that I am with you always even to the ends of the world," I pray in Jesus' name that your blood should follow through every artery, every vein, every muscle. God, I pray right now that you will restore, restore what the enemy has tried to steal. And Satan we rebuke you right now, we rebuke you even trying to disturb this body of God. In the name of Jesus, get in our hands, God. Restore everything, Jesus. I pray that you restore even things that she thinks she's forgotten and enemy when you try to tell her that she can't remember some things we rebuke you in the name of Jesus. We thank you for the labor that she and her husband have done for 60 years. God, you have not forgotten them. "Lo, I'm with you always," and I pray in the name of Jesus that your blood should flow through every vein in this body in the name of Jesus. We are so glad that we don't have to beg you and I pray in Jesus' name now that you would just remind*

her of the things she even gave up Lord, not even count it as worthy to be your child. But God she was not doing that as a payback but she and her husband were just being open to you. In the name of Jesus. To this body we curse every disease that has been tempting her body, in the name of Jesus. We curse it right now in Jesus' name. We rebuke it right now in the name of Jesus. What a miracle. It is not a miracle to you because that's just who you are. You are a miracle worker. We call it a miracle but to you it's just Jesus. That's who you are and I pray in Jesus' name right now that the restoration of this wonderful woman shall begin right now, in the name of Jesus. All the other prayers that the other saints have prayed God, we pray that you would just put them collectively together, in Jesus' name. Let oh God, let her have a dance to her spirit, in the name of Jesus. Hallelujah! Flow through this body. Take away all the fear, take away that fear and bad memories of anything God. You've done it for me time and time again. And God by faith would we see this healing. In the name of Jesus. Hallelujah.

As the prayer and medications continued, I began to improve quite a bit, and my walking quickly improved to the point where I would walk a mile each evening. God also opened lots of doors for me in the USA to continue to minister to my friends back in Japan and in the USA. Whether they were Christians or not, I was concerned for each of them. During this time, I met Kathy Brubacher, who came to help me with so many things like regular correspondence. After graduating from seminary in Japan, she came to America and she home schooled her children until junior high. She has been a great help to me because of her excellent translation skills. This enabled me to catch up with many of my contacts in Japan. Now, they could contact me by email and snail mail so we could keep in touch in many ways.

During this time, I also kept a busy schedule at a time when others my age were well into retirement. I hosted guests from the USA, wrote an advice column on the internet, counseled Japanese and expatriates with family problems, and was a grandmother to my beloved grandchildren, showering them with gifts and encouraging emails.

Mom was always there, and though a full-time missionary with English classes, ladies' meetings, and cooking classes, she was always available and made time for us. I remember going out for an evening jog for a mile or two with Mom when I was a teenager. Mom had an amazing Norwegian horse sense to give us lots of freedom to go places and take trips. And as we would leave, she would leave with us the words that would ring in our heads the whole time, "Remember Whose you are and Whom you serve." Mom was the one I went to if I had a problem. She would always listen. She is the living example of the love of Christ to me. No one is more loving and giving than her. If I were asked who most exemplifies Christ on earth, it would be Mom.

–Bobb Joseph

Perhaps the biggest crisis of my life happened in January of 2017 when Kenny passed away. In the last couple of years, even though he had had hip and knee surgeries and heart stents put in, he still was having trouble with his knees and it was getting harder and harder for him to get around. So we scheduled two surgeries—one for knee replacement, and another for his hip that was to take place in early 2017. But he didn't make it that far.

I knew that Kenny was very thankful toward me but he didn't always show it, cautious about giving any kind of compliment to people. But two weeks before he passed away, one day, out of the blue he turned to me and said, "Has anyone ever told you what a wonderful wife you are?" I look back on that now and think what a wonderful memory that is to have about him.

"There aren't enough musical notes or letters in the alphabet to express how grateful I am to God for giving Mom to us. Wherever I go, whatever I do, her words, expressed over a lifetime with grace and love, guide me"

–Mark Joseph

Mark and his family had celebrated Christmas with us and then gone to Japan for two weeks, and my niece Beth was staying with us in their absence. Kenny was sitting in his chair waiting for his breakfast, and suddenly began talking in Japanese to Beth. I said to him, "You know, Kenny, Beth doesn't understand Japanese."

Beth thought it was strange, too, and she called Bobb and wondered if she should call an ambulance. Bobb suggested Dad first rest a bit, but when Kenny woke up, this odd behavior continued. Beth called the ambulance and they arrived and Kenny now spoke to them in Japanese. We knew something was seriously wrong. In the ambulance Kenny followed commands but stopped talking and went into a coma. We later learned that he was suffering a massive brain hemorrhage that was causing this confusion. He spent his last moments speaking the language of the nation he loved and had served for sixty-plus years.

He spent two days in the hospital unconscious, but we felt strongly that he could hear us, so as family and friends gathered around him in the hospital we sang, prayed, and reminisced with him. Six-year-old Emilyn found a scrap of paper and wrote on it, "I love you grandpa. Have fun in heaven." So, even though we wanted to keep him, it seems like it was God's timing, and we had to accept that though we are lonesome and miss him. The memorial service was outstanding. Many people came and spoke and sang at it.

Both my and Kenny's lives have been full of unexpected surprises, joys, and sorrows, but through it all, we have clung to God and each other and showed the staying power that comes from a life that is animated by the resurrection power of Jesus Christ.

It's taken some getting used to, being without my life partner of sixty years. On top of that, I lost my last brother Orvin to a heart attack nine months later. So I am now entering a new season of being a widow, but I am close to family and friends and continue to rejoice that through many hardships, challenges, joys, and victories, God continues to guide my life, and I continue to serve him to the best of my ability.

I hope you've learned a thing or two through my story, and that God will use it to inspire you to do even greater things for Him. God's not finished with me yet, and I intend to use whatever time He has left for me to serve Him with all my strength. Through it all, I've found that, as the title of this book suggests, we can either be dragged down by life or rise above the challenges we face. Three hundred sixty-five times in the Bible God encourages us to "fear not"–one for each day. I've found that love and optimism and hope have provided me with great strength to face the challenges God has allowed in my life, and through it all, He has been faithful. Most important of all, if you haven't done so already I ask you to receive the gift of life that's Jesus Christ. He's a wonderful Savior, who will give you life abundant if you will bring your sins to his feet, repent of them, and ask Him to come into your heart. Then you too will know for yourself God's power in your life. He loves you and has a wonderful plan for your life.

APPENDIX

Selected Poems by Lila Joseph

IT'S NOT TOO LATE

· · · · · · · · · · · · · · · · · · · ·

Wow! am I ever glad to be here!
But I must confess I was surprised that
You called me.
You know, I'm not SO old yet.

I never walked on gold before;
A couple of gold jewelry chains
and some rings were about it.

The sky is so blue and clear;
Beauty and orderliness everywhere.

I know some of those people over there.
From our church.
They don't seem to particularly notice me.
Oh well, I didn't pay much attention to them either.
When we were near each other.

But Jesus, You welcomed me.
I'm glad for that.
I can tell You're happy to have me here.
Still, You seem kinda reserved.
Maybe even sad.

Strange. Some things are dawning on me.
Now I realize that most of the people I worked with
Won't be here.
I can't believe how utterly self-centered I was.

I thought it was stalwart to just "live" like a Christian.
Just warming a pew on Sundays.
I knew I was born-again,

I remember the time I asked You to come into my heart.
But my faith was weak.
I see that now.
Sometimes my Bible lay unread for days.
You know, magazines, papers, TV.
Always beckoning.

And praying!
Well, Lord, you know there can't be many here because of my prayers.
A few quick "God bless"es while sailing down the freeway
In between gulps of coffee
Were about it.

There's no excuse either.

I can't remember how many times our pastor
spoke on prayer.
And YOU nudged me, too, Lord.
I was so caught up in day-to-day living.

I planned to pray more.
To help people more.
To ask YOU what You really wanted.
Some day. Some day.
I just forgot how short life can be.
In reality I forgot the purpose You had for me.
Now I see that it wasn't to "get ahead."
Or to keep up with even the
Christian Joneses.
Or to just have the latest "things."

I was to be Your witness.
To take Your place.
That was the last speech You gave to
Your disciples.
And to all Your children.

There's no use asking if I can go back;
Back to help my family.
They were always glad when I kept my "religion" to myself.

Back to the office.
Don sure isn't ready. Neither is Jack.
Or Carl, for that matter. Or Alice.
I know I could have made all of them listen.
I could have shown more interest.
Been more caring.

There wasn't much "cup of cold water" business from MY life.

But, like You said, if I did go back
They probably wouldn't listen.
They'd think I was a ghost.
Or deranged.

This is really getting to me, Lord.
Now I know why You were sad when You greeted me.
I'm glad You said You'd wipe away our tears.
There wouldn't be enough Kleenex in all of Heaven
To comfort me and others who've lived just for ourselves.

Thank you for Praying

This morning I was burdened,
I couldn't even pray, I said, "My Lord, I don't know why,
But I don't know what to say."

How could I have the wisdom
To know just how to ask,
The problem was too big for me
My need I couldn't mask.

I read my Bible, did my work,
Both listlessly and slow,

I just couldn't reach the Throne Room
For my soul had lost its glow.

So I lifted up my problem,
Gave it all to Him to mend--
How even He could sort it out
I couldn't comprehend.

The day wore on and tasks were done
I move in robot-style,
When suddenly I sensed a change,
From inside I could smile.

Dark presssure was all lifted,
My mind was calm and still,
The change was so dramatic
It went beyond my will.

I pondered what had happened
And then I clearly knew
That God had touched some tender heart
I wonder, was it you?

He'd asked for one to stand up strong
To pray and praise and rout
The enemy who like a flood
Had moved in all about.

"Oh my Father, thank you!
For the one who prayed for me,
Please give that one a special touch
Who served so faithfully."

SURPRISE WELCOME IN HEAVEN

·····················

Thanks, Jesus, for such a warm welcome!
And for wiping away my tears!
It's been kinda rough.
But now I can see that it was worth it!
I can't believe this dazzling beauty
All around.
The sky. The grass. The flowers.
So vivid. Striking. Breath-taking.
The buildings. And the music.
But mostly I'm glad to see You.
I can never thank You enough for finding me
When I had gone astray.
You turned me around.
It was different from then on.
Hard lots of times.
But I kept reading Your Word
And talking to You.
You kept Your end of the bargain
With peace. Power. Guidance.
I couldn't have gone it alone.
At first everyone made fun of me.
But they gave up.
You kept reminding me that I was in warfare.
That my short stay on earth was not to be a settling in.
I remember once when I was downcast
You led me to Hebrews
Where I read
"For this world is not our home;
We are looking to our everlasting home in heaven."
So here I am. Thank you, Jesus.
I'll say that over and over I know.
But who's that?

Looks like he's waiting for me.
In fact, all those people seem to be waiting.
Oh, I recognize a lot of them.
My family.
Yes, they finally came to You.
One by one.
I'm so anxious to talk to each one!
But Lord, I don't know any of the others.
That one. Waiting.
He was? He was that salesman I shared You with?
And her--the one I gave that tract to?
And witnessed to
At the supermarket? She was crying, I remember.
And those people--our neighbors from our old place.
After we moved I never saw them again.
But I prayed for them.
Sure I remember praying for the people in the airplanes
Going overhead.

Naturally I didn't hear anything about them
A lot of them must have come to You.
But Lord, You know I never went
To Africa
Or South America
Or Japan.
How could those people be welcoming me?
Well sure, I prayed and helped the missionaries
As much as I could
But still I felt insignificant
Their job seemed more important.
Sure, I know they couldn't have done it alone.
Wow! Everyone's so beautiful
Really? They weren't when they came?
Each one seems bubbling over to tell their story to me
And I'm sure I can understand them here!
But, as happy as I am,
I'm sad, too.

I could have helped more
I could have prayed more
You've done so much for me
And I've really done so little.

CPSIA information can be obtained
at www.ICGtesting.com
Printed in the USA
LVHW04s0206290618
582236LV00002B/2/P